S0-BRM-843

745.92 Mar   MPS

Martin, Laura C.

The art and craft of
  pounding flowers   7/01

The Art and Craft of

Pounding Flowers

The Art and Craft of

Pounding Flowers

laura c. martin

Moline Public Library
MOLINE, ILLINOIS

3 0050 04565 2137

QVC PUBLISHING

QVC Publishing, Inc.
Jill Cohen, Vice President and Publisher
Ellen Bruzelius, General Manager
Sarah Butterworth, Editorial Director
Karen Murgolo, Director of Acquisitions and Rights
Cassandra Reynolds, Publishing Assistant

Produced by Fair Street Productions, Inc.
Project Director: Susan Wechsler
Designer: Barbara Balch
Editor: Cheryl Tetreau

Illustrations by Laura C. Martin
Photography by Cameron and Laura C. Martin except for the following pages
by Steven Mays: ii, 2 (top left, bottom right), 22 (top left, bottom right), 32, 33,
34, 36, 42 (top left, bottom right), 45, 47, 48, 50, 52, 57, 59, 60, 67, 69, 73,
75, 79, 81, 82 (top left, bottom right), 85, 86, 89, 91, 92, 99, 100, 102 (top left,
bottom right), 107, 108, 111, 114, 117, 123, 125, 126, 127, 128 (top left, bottom
right), 131, 132, 135, 137, 149

Q Publishing and colophon are trademarks of QVC Publishing, Inc.

Copyright © 2001 Laura C. Martin

All rights reserved. No part of this book may be reproduced or transmitted in any
form or by any means, electronic or mechanical, including photocopying, recording,
or by any information storage and retrieval system, without permission in writing
from the publisher.

Published by QVC Publishing, Inc.
50 Main Street, Mt. Kisco, New York 10549

QVC Publishing books are available at special discounts when purchased in bulk
for premiums and sales promotions as well as for fund-raising or educational use.
Special editions or book excerpts can be created to specifications. For details,
contact the address below:
QVC Publishing
50 Main Street, Suite 201
Mount Kisco, New York 10549

Manufactured in England

ISBN: 1-928998-41-0
Library-of-Congress catalogue information available on request.

First Edition

10 9 8 7 6 5 4 3 2 1

Contents

Acknowledgments

Growing up in a family of artists was sometimes challenging but always interesting. But the support, enthusiasm and endless ideas that I received from my family for this project touched my heart. Special thanks goes to: my daughter, Cameron Martin, for her wonderful photographs; to my son, Dave Martin, for his unquenchable enthusiasm for the entire project; to my mother, Lois Coogle, for her advice on paints, finishes, and suggestions for various projects; to my father, Ken Coogle, for his advice on hammers and for keeping my hammers polished(!); to my sister, Sharon Coogle, for her excellent suggestions for design and ideas for many of the paper crafts; and to my niece, Christine Coogle, for testing out some of the projects from an 8-year-old point of view. Thanks, also, to my friend Renae Smith for sharing her boundless creativity and for her help in making the flower fairies.

Thank you to Jill Cohen and Ellen Bruzelius at QVC Publishing for their continuous and unflagging support for this project; to Barbara Balch for her beautiful and creative book design; to Cheryl Tetreau for her editing mastery; to Steven Mays for his excellent photographs of the projects; and to Susan Wechsler for being the nucleus that kept us all on track and on schedule.

Introduction

Like any new craft, rumors and whispers about hammering flowers onto cloth came to me from different sources. The idea was intriguing, though my first attempt at this craft was a disaster—I'm surprised I even tried again. I pounded a partially dried hydrangea leaf onto a piece of copy paper and it looked like a squished bug. But then I hammered a tiny viola onto watercolor paper and the result was stunning. I've hardly put my hammer down since.

If you can hammer a nail, you can be an artist! Welcome to the new craft of making lasting and beautiful botanical impressions with little more than a hammer, fabric or paper, and plant materials. I'm not aware of any other craft that offers so many creative opportunities and can be done by such a wide variety of people—from preschoolers to graduate art students to the elderly population. This is a craft that is mysterious, yet simple; it is also failproof and, at the same time, challenging.

The basic technique can be described in only a few words: Simply pick a flower, place it on paper or fabric, cover with a paper towel, and hammer away. The results are astounding—and instant. Many plants transfer perfectly onto material, complete with vibrant colors and tiny details. There is no waiting, no mixing paint, no applying ink. Some plants, such as little Johnny-jump-ups, transfer so perfectly you almost need a magnifying glass to see all the details. Other plants, such as impatiens, come out looking more like an impressionistic painting.

Although this craft is literally easy enough for a preschooler to do, it also offers variations that will attract and challenge even the most experienced artist. Each plant transfers in a unique way, and even the same kind of plant will transfer with varying results, depending upon how mature the leaves or flowers are, what type of material or paper is used, and whether or not the fabric was pretreated before hammering. All of these factors influence the look of the final plant image.

Writing this book has been all about trial and error and discovery, for each flower and leaf brought new surprises. Some of the impressions I created went straight into the trash can, but others came out so well that I used them to adorn clothing such as blouses and scarves, to create art suitable for framing or decorating useful items such as tablecloths and tote bags. My "research" led me to try 60 different plants, flowers, and leaves (see "Plant Guide" on pages 154–174 for a full listing). The result is this book—a treasure trove of information for crafters.

You may wonder why a craft as easy as pounding flowers would warrant a book. My answer is a simple one: While the basic technique is undeniably easy, the variations are so endless they can be overwhelming. Which plants work best? What fabrics and papers work best? How do you make the image long-lasting? Can you wash the fabric impressions? You'll find the answers to these questions, and many more, in the pages that follow.

This book gets you started, offering ideas for plants that give you good impressions, the best materials to impress them on, and instructions for making crafts with the materials you have decorated. Some of these projects take only a few minutes to do, while others are works of art that take months to finish. In addition,

numerous photographs show you the colors and kinds of impressions you can expect to get from many common flowers and leaves, taking much of the guess work out of the craft.

I've filled this book with information on the art of hammering flowers, and my hope is that you will use it as a springboard to stimulate your own creativity. Start here, with my basic techniques and instructions, then venture out and try new flowers, using them in new ways. While it's fun to have and give items made from your hammered art, it is the process of creation that is the true gift of this craft, for it allows everyone, almost without exception, to become an artist. So read through the basic instructions, take a look at some of the projects, then give it a try—you'll never have more fun with a hammer!

Get Ready

CHOOSING AND USING PLANTS • CHOOSING FABRICS, PAPER, AND OTHER MATERIALS • TOOLS OF THE TRADE MAKING SAMPLE CARDS

Gather Your Materials

*T*here's not much equipment involved in making a beautiful botanical impression—basically all you need are a hammer and a flower! But the hammered images you make will be so stunning you'll want to use them to make items to wear, to give away, or to decorate your home. In this chapter, you'll learn how to choose plants, paper, fabrics, and tools to create lasting impressions.

Choosing and Using Plants

*T*his book includes enough information about plants to last a lifetime, but part of the fun of the craft is to try out new plants in new ways. Of course, you will never be able to try out all the plants in the world, but that means there will always be delightful surprises awaiting you as you

< Fresh dogwood and wisteria blossoms transfer beautifully onto fabric for one-of-a-kind creations.

do this craft. I am still surprised by how some plant materials turn out, though I have tested hundreds of blossoms and leaves and can usually guess which plants will work and which ones will not.

For example, I waited and waited for my purple coneflower to put out its purple-pink petals only to find that, when hammered, they turned brown almost immediately on all types of

- Choose flowers that have thin, brilliantly colored petals. The lighter the flower color, the lighter the transfer will be. For example, transfers from yellow flowers usually do not hold their colors well (the exceptions are coreopsis and marigold).

- Don't hammer plants that are fleshy and full of liquid.

- Don't hammer plants that have a hard or thick center without taking it apart first.

- Don't hammer leaves that are shiny with a waxy surface, such as magnolia or holly.

- Hammer petals, leaves, etc. in a single layer. If you hammer multiple layers of plant material at one time, the smashed material will resemble a splash of mud.

- Start by placing the side with the most interest (color, venation, pattern, etc.) face down on your material to be hammered. If you don't like the results, get another leaf or petal and try hammering with the opposite side down.

- Be certain that your plant material is completely dry. If it has rained recently (or if you've just watered the garden) take a paper towel and gently press on the plant until all moisture has been absorbed.

- Test and practice on a scrap of paper or fabric before you start a project.

fabrics. And hydrangea—what a disappointment! These beautiful blue flowers are perfect for dried flower crafts, but when they're hammered the color fades instantly. But kudzu, on the other hand, was a remarkable success. Good thing that pesky weed is good for *something!*

FLOWERS

The flowers you choose to hammer will be those that are (1) readily available to you, (2) ones you want for a particular project, or (3) so beautiful or fascinating you just have to see how they hammer. If you become caught up in enthusiasm for this craft, you will, undoubtedly, hammer many impressions that make you groan with disappointment—but you'll pound many, many more that make you gasp with pleasure. And that is part of the fun of the craft.

Even though it's difficult to tell exactly how a particular flower will turn out, there are many characteristics that poundable flowers seem to share. Remember, these are generalizations. There is no way to accurately predict what kind of impression an untested plant produces. Some leaves and flowers present a stunning impression when you least expect it. But, in general, follow the guidelines in "Hammering How-To," on page 4.

WORKING WITH FLOWERS

Some flowers, such as impatiens, verbena, or phlox, can simply be put down on a material, covered with a paper towel, and hammered to make a perfect impression. Most flowers, however, need a little "prep" work to produce the best results. There are two reasons for this. First, most flowers have depth and layers that make them beautiful to look at "on the vine" but difficult to get a clear transfer from. Whenever you use a hammer to get an image, you must pound one layer at a time, otherwise you'll get a smeared design because of the excess plant tissue. For example, chrysanthemum petals hammer beautifully one at a time, but if you put the entire blossom down and hammer it, you'll end up with just a smashed mass of plant material that resembles mud.

Second, many flowers grow around a central axis that is thick, hard, or fleshy—none of which transfer cleanly.

Many blossoms, such as lilies and iris, have petals that are thin at the ends, but get thicker toward the center of the blossom. You can either simply cut off the fleshy parts, if the petal shape is conducive to that, or you can put the fleshy parts between two paper towels and gently squeeze out as much moisture as possible before you hammer.

Although there are numerous types of flowers, each of which should be treated differently, there are also general guidelines that make it easier to get a lasting impression, no matter

what kind of flower you are working with. Use the "Flower Guidelines" on pages 6–7 to guide you. Keep in mind that whenever you need to take a flower apart, keep an additional intact flower close by so you can remember how it looks in the original. This is particularly true of flowers such as wisteria or iris in which you are using only a small part of the entire blossom and want a representation rather than a reproduction.

TOP TEN FLOWERS

1. Lobelia
2. Bee balm
3. Verbena
4. Marigold
5. Pansy / viola
6. Coreopsis
7. Phlox
8. Nigella (love in a mist)
9. Impatiens
10. Cosmos

Viola made the list even though you really have to work with the flower. It fades after a few months, but the transfer is so incredible, I had to include it.

FLOWER GUIDELINES

Here are general guidelines to follow when choosing flowers for pounding.
For detailed information about specific pounding techniques, see Chapter 2.

TYPE OF FLOWER

HOW TO USE

Daisy-type flowers.
These are comprised
of a circle of petals
(botanically known as
ray flowers) surround-
ing a center composed
of tiny disc flowers.
Flowers that fall into
this general category
include coreopsis,
gaillardia, calendula,
aster, old-fashioned
single roses, and
zinnia.

First try hammering the entire blossom
without pulling it apart. Cosmos, for
example, hammers well this way. Tape
down the petals or hold firmly with a
paper towel, then tap on all the petals,
increasing the pressure of the hammering until you have a
good transfer. Begin to hammer the center part, gently at
first, then with more pressure.

If the center part is too fleshy or hard, pull the petals
off and hammer these separately. To do this, carefully pull the petals from the center, either with your
fingers or with tweezers. To keep the petals in a perfect circle, tape each one down or hammer each one
separately. In addition to creating a full circular
impression, you can also do a "side view" where you
use only half the number of petals, arranged as if
you were looking at the flower from the side.

**Flowers with
mounds of petals.**
Many flowers have
several layers of
petals, resulting in a
mounded blossom.
Because they have an
abundance of petals, a
single blossom can be
taken apart to be used
to make several flower
designs. Flowers that
fall into this category
include carnation,
chrysanthemum, rose,
peony, and many types
of dahlia.

Pull petals off gently, and reassemble
on the material to be pounded.
Hammer one at a time or tape in place.

Pay attention to the
different lengths of the
petals. Use all the same length
petals in your design, or alternate
long and short ones.

Remember that spaces
are as important as images when creating a design, and
it's best to allow plenty of blank spaces around each petal.
(See "Creating a Pleasing Design" on pages 35–37.)

Unusual-shaped blossoms. Flowers such as iris or bee balm have unique configurations of blossoms.

Take apart the flower and reassemble on your material to give a good representation of the original. For example, bee balm has several tubular flowers surrounded by colorful bracts.

Hammer a few of each, with flowers pointing upward and bracts pointing downward, as a representation of the full blossom.

Tubular flowers. Many flowers, such as petunia, phlox, and vinca, have petals that are connected at the base in a tubular configuration.

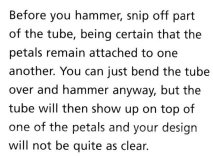

Before you hammer, snip off part of the tube, being certain that the petals remain attached to one another. You can just bend the tube over and hammer anyway, but the tube will then show up on top of one of the petals and your design will not be quite as clear.

Clusters of blossoms. Many flowers, such as verbena and wisteria, grow in clusters but have individual blossoms that make great transfers.

Some can be plucked and hammered without any prep work at all. Others, such as wisteria, need to be cut and spliced and put back together to get a good representation. When you are making a transfer of a bundle or clump of flowers, it's best to hammer the stem in first and then replace the blossoms along the stem.

While fern impressions turn brown after a few weeks, they are wonderful for making iron-on transfers or for enhancing with paint. (See "Enhancing the Images" on pages 33–34.)

LEAVES

Choose leaves with interest—nice vein patterns, pleasing colors, or ones with interesting shapes. Many leaves don't have much pigment and often that color squirts to the sides rather than making a nice overall impression. Unless you need, or want, to be botanically correct, you can remove the leaves from a flower that you are working with and replace them with leaves that make a better impression. And keep in mind that young leaves release their pigments more readily and have more detailed shapes than older leaves.

Autumn leaves bring a whole new dimension to the craft. The colors are stunning and exciting to work with and the shapes are magnificent, though many dry as they turn colors and don't have enough moisture to make a good impression.

Many fleshy plants may seem to be unsuitable for hammering, but can be used, if they are treated before you hammer them. The most common example is a thick leaf, such as that from a flowering cabbage. If you just pick it and put it down on fabric, it will squirt pigments out in a most unseemly manner. However, if you press the leaf overnight in a plant press or even between paper towels in a thick book, the leaf will usually have lost enough moisture to make a good impression. Obviously, timing here is important. If you leave it in too long, too much moisture will be lost and you can't hammer it at all; wait too short a time and the leaf will still squirt when hammered.

STEMS

Stems are difficult to work with; many are tubular, so when you hammer them you will get two stripes of green. Some are also full of sap (with good reason—that's their job!), so when you hammer them, they squirt out on the sides and fade quickly. There are two ways to deal with these kinds of stems. One, you can avoid them and look for a plant that gives you a nice, clean line. I found that vetch stems gave a good transfer, as did the green stems of nandina. If these are not available to you, experiment with plants that you have access to. The alternative is to work with difficult stems by taking a sharp knife and splitting the stem in two. Then take a paper towel and wick as much moisture from the stem as you can before you hammer it.

ROOTS

Roots can be very effective, and sometimes you'll want to include them in your designs. For example, fern roots proved to make perfect hair for the flower figures on page 74. But not all roots make good impressions—you should only use roots with pigment or ones that are evenly covered with dirt. I'm not opposed to using dirt as a pigment, but you need to make sure that you don't get clumps and smears of brown; what you're after are the delicate fine lines of the root itself.

To find good roots, just dig up a few plants (start with the weeds!). You'll find that a surprising number of roots are white and will not transfer well; and many weed roots are either too difficult to pull up or are wiry and don't release their pigments easily. As with all other kinds of transfers, experiment with the plants most readily available to you.

> ### TOP TEN LEAVES
>
> 1. Asparagus fern (not a true fern)
> 2. Vetch
> 3. Sweet gum
> 4. Japanese maple
> 5. Redbud
> 6. Caladium
> 7. Sourwood
> 8. Wild grape
> 9. Nandina
> 10. Ferns—all kinds

Leaves, such as (from left) nandina, sourwood, and sweet gum, offer a variety of shapes and colors perfect for hammering.

Choosing Fabrics, Paper, and Other Materials

I've found that fabrics and heavy papers are the most satisfactory materials for making hammered images. You can also make impressions on leather, though it is not so easy a task. A third option is to use polymer clay, such as Sculpey, Fimo, or Cernit. It can be easily manipulated to take many different plant and flower impressions.

FABRIC

Although I prefer to use natural fibers (cotton, linen, silk, and wool), synthetic fabrics will also take impressions with varying results. To eliminate as many variables as possible and to increase the predictable beauty of your results, stick to natural fibers for most of your projects. If you want to use synthetic blends for a particular project, just be certain to test out the fabric with the plant material you intend to use.

Because you want your images to show up as brilliantly as possible, you should hammer them onto a pale colored background. Although my first choice of color is white or off-white, you can also hammer images on pastel colors. If you choose colored fabric, keep in mind that the color intensity of the image itself will change. For example, bright green leaves change color when hammered on yellow instead of white, and come out yet another color when hammered on blue. Some of this color change has to do with the actual color of the fabric showing through the image; some of it is a result of tricks to the eye that occur when you place two colors next to one another. I strongly suggest that you practice hammering on various colored materials before you plunge in and choose one color to work with.

It would seem logical to assume that white flowers will show up beautifully on dark fabrics, but, unfortunately, this isn't true. White blossoms do not contain pigment, so their petals are simply absorbed into the darkness of the fabric. The result is disappointing.

Regardless of color, there is no one fabric that is "best." One plant gives a perfect impression on linen, while another looks better on wool. The plant and fabric you choose depend on the type of image you want. Each plant discussed in this book was tested on four natural fibers, pretreated with alum (see pages 23–24 for information on pretreating fabrics). The chart at right describes the fabrics I used for testing purposes.

FABRIC

COMMENTS

Cotton (with grape)

The sample is a medium weight, plain-weave cotton cloth, similar to a broadcloth, with little texture.

Twill and canvas, in general, took impressions very well, but were unsuitable for iron-on transfers (see pages 29–31) because of the distinct weave of the cloth. Batiste was good for many flowers but was too thin to hold the pigments of others. Cotton flannel also took impressions very well but has limited usefulness, as it is a difficult fabric to use in home décor. If you use this for decorated sleepwear, be certain to use iron-on transfer decorations so you can wash it. Test the transfer on the fabric before you use either of them in a final project.

Silk (with sourwood)

The sample is China silk, very thin and flimsy. I chose this because China silk is used to make many "ready-to-decorate" items, such as scarves, ties, and eyeglass cases, found in the silk-painting department of crafts stores. It was the most difficult of the sample fabrics to work with, because it was so thin it sometimes could not hold the pigments. However, I came to love the soft and fuzzy impressions it did make and used it for creating many elegant items. A few plants left a bright, stunning impression, all the more special because of their rarity. The choice of plants and cover materials is particularly important with this fabric.

There are many different types of silks, including satins, organza, taffeta, velvet, jersey, chiffon, and brocade, most of which were unsuitable for hammering art. Crepe de chine, however, held the impressions beautifully and is wonderful to use for making fine garments. Raw silk, used in the summer shawl on pages 88–90, was difficult to use because it had a surface that didn't allow many of the plant pigments to penetrate, but those that did left a lovely impression.

FABRIC	COMMENTS

Wool (with kudzu)

The sample is a smooth worsted wool. Unlike the other sample fabrics, which are white, this is a light cream color. It took almost all the impressions beautifully, resulting in deep, rich colors, almost always a little darker than impressions on the other sample cloths.

Wool falls into two categories—woolens, which are soft with a rough or fuzzy texture, and worsteds, which are smooth, strong, and more lustrous. Only worsted wools are suitable for taking the impressions. Wool crepe, which is a worsted, was a little difficult to work with because of the uneven weave, but took some impressions beautifully. It's a nice fabric for scarves and other accessories.

Linen (with dahlia)

The sample has straight, even weaving with fine knobs. It was a good-quality linen with a high thread-per-inch count, though it can't compare to ancient Egyptian mummy cloth, which has 500 threads per inch! (Today's fine cotton percale sheets have 220 threads per inch.) Although the texture of the linen is a little difficult to work with, the bright, lively colors obtained from the impressions made all the trouble worthwhile. Linen wrinkles easily, but irons beautifully after the mordant bath.

Handkerchief linen, a light, soft linen cloth used to make fine clothing and undergarments, is great for hammered art.

MORDANTS FOR PRETREATING FABRIC

Crafters who dye cloth pretreat their yarn and cloth with a substance called a mordant. The word mordant actually comes from the Latin word *mordere*, which means "to bite," or "to fasten onto." The materials that have been treated with a mordant are better able to absorb pigments from the dye.

Mordanting techniques are used to help make the hammered impressions transfer true to color and last longer. Though some plants, such as blue hydrangea, will not hammer true to color no matter what you do to the fabric, other plant colors are greatly enhanced by the mordanting process. Red and pink flowers, in particular, need the chemical changes that occur through mordanting to transfer their tones and shades. Having said that, I must emphasize that mordanting fabric is both time consuming and bothersome, and may not be necessary for all projects. I strongly suggest that you practice hammering your plants on a piece of untreated fabric first and, if you like the results, proceed with untreated fabric rather than going through the effort of mordanting. If you decide to give mordanting a try, read on.

Although there are several mordants commonly used by dyers, for the purposes of hammered art, alum and cream of tartar are all you need. Alum takes well to all four natural fibers—cotton, wool, silk, and linen—and is the least caustic and mildest of the mordants. Even so, be sure to avoid direct contact with the mordant bath by wearing rubber gloves. Though alum is a natural substance and will not harm the soil, dispose of the spent alum carefully. It can be safely poured out on the ground; just take care to keep it away from septic tanks, water sources, pets, or places where children play.

When you use alum, the measurements don't have to be precise (a dozen different dyers will give you a dozen different recipes for an alum bath). Just be sure that you don't use too much alum, particularly with wool, or it will make the fabric slightly sticky. You can only use the mordant bath once, and should prepare a new bath for each additional piece of cloth.

Alum can sometimes be found in the grocery store or at a pharmacy and is readily available at crafts stores (look in the fabric-painting department). Cream of tartar, though not a mordant in itself, is added to the alum bath to allow the pigments to be taken up more evenly and to slightly brighten the colors. Cream of tartar is the same substance that you buy for cooking and is found in the baking section of the grocery store. If you do a lot of hammered art, purchase this in bulk from a craft store or mail-order catalog.

MORDANTING EQUIPMENT

Here's what you'll need to mordant your fabrics. See "Pretreating Fabrics" on pages 23–24 for step-by-step directions.

- Large nonreactive pans (unchipped enamel or stainless steel; use ones with flat bottoms so your fabric wrinkles as little as possible during mordanting)
- Large stainless steel bowl
- Stove or hot plate
- Long stirring rods or long-handled plastic spoons
- 2-quart pitcher
- Measuring cup
- Measuring spoons
- Kitchen scales
- Rubber gloves
- Apron
- Waterproof marker for identifying mordant equipment

- Colors on wool seemed to be darker and more intense than on other fabrics.

- Linen took the impressions well and the colors were brighter and truer than on the other fabrics. The pigments were not always absorbed evenly on the rough weave of the cloth, though, and sometimes gave the impression of being striped.

- Colors on cotton, particularly reds and pinks, were often muddy looking even when the fabric had been mordanted. Blues and purples generally stayed true to color.

- Silk produced the palest, least distinct impressions, but the colors were clear and the overall effect lovely.

PAPER

It's more difficult to get a good impression on paper than it is on fabric, but some plants did transfer well to paper. For the most part, heavy, absorbent paper, such as that made for watercolor painting, is more satisfactory than lightweight paper. Mulberry paper, though thin, takes many transfers well and is very useful for making items such as endpapers for books or lining for an envelope. Handmade paper, whether purchased or homemade, is good for making impressions. But thicker specialty papers, such as bark or vellum, do not take the transfers well.

Some plants will transfer beautifully even to inexpensive white paper. Just don't allow cheap paper to be your benchmark for whether a particular plant will transfer successfully or not, because this material is one of the most difficult to hammer on.

LEATHER

It's difficult, but possible, to transfer images to leather. A precious few plants yield enough pigment to make a good impression. Ultra-suede is slightly easier to work with than treated leather, but not much. White Ultra-suede is probably the best bet. When you work with these materials, be sure to use the side that looks the most absorbent—the side without a finish or coating. If this is a material that greatly interests you, buy a small amount and practice with available plants. I found that deep-purple dahlia and passionflower vine leaves made the best impressions on leather.

POLYMER CLAY

Craft clays, such as Sculpey, Fimo, and Cernit, are fun to decorate with plants. The clay remains malleable until it is baked in the oven, so you can press blossoms and leaves into the clay and bake them right in. There are great possibilities for combining clay crafts and hammered art to make jewelry and home décor items. (See "Beyond Paper and Fabric: Working with Polymer Clay" on pages 38–39 for details.)

Tools of the Trade

In addition to the plant material and the fabric, paper, leather, or clay that you've chosen to work with, you'll need some tools to help you produce your pounded images. The most important, of course, is a hammer. Then there is the hammering surface to consider, as well as what material you'll use to cover the plant as you pound. But don't worry, it's not that complicated, and I've taken away most of the guesswork for you.

HAMMERS

Needless to say, I have several hammers. I keep one in the car and have others stashed away in handy places, just in case I suddenly come upon a flower that I want to hammer. My favorite hammer is my little $6.99 hardware store model. It's nothing special, just a small, light-weight hammer with a flat metal head. Many people quiz me about the kind of hammer I use, thinking that a craft as unique as pounding flowers must need a magical tool, but it just isn't so. I've tried ball peen hammers, sledge hammers, tack hammers, curved-claw hammers, ripping hammers, wooden mallets, rubber mallets, plastic mallets, and a variety of other hammering tools including rocks, but an old-fashioned hammer seems to do the trick.

Just be sure to choose a hammer that has a flat surface, rather than a rounded one, and a metal head. A mallet works fine for some plants, but in general, a regular hammer works best. One note: if you are working with young children or older adults, get as lightweight a hammer as you can find. It does take some strength, even to hammer a flower!

If you're on a field trip with kids or taking a nature walk, you might be tempted to just pick up a rock and start pounding. But I've had little success with this. The problem with using a rock is that it doesn't have a perfectly flat surface, and it has to be quite small to get the pounds-per-inch pressure necessary for a good impression. You can get some impressions this way, though, so try it out for yourself and have fun with it. Just keep in mind that you'll get much better results if you use a hammer.

HAMMERING SURFACE

The choice of how you sandwich your fabric and plants for hammering—what you put underneath and on top—is surprisingly critical for making a good impression. Your goal is to alter the absorbency of the materials to produce the crispest lines and to get the greatest amount of pigment possible on your paper or fabric. There are many variables that affect this, including the hammering surface, cover materials, and the type, age, and maturity of the plant material.

The best hammering surface is a flat wooden chopping board covered with a double layer of

HAMMER ETIQUETTE

- Do not hammer in a hotel room, especially early in the morning or late at night. Other guests will not appreciate it, no matter how beautiful your images come out. If you are staying in a hotel, go out by the pool or find someplace outside where you can make as much noise as you need to without bothering anyone. The same rule applies if you are a guest in a home.

- Do not pick flowers or plants in a park or designated wilderness or protected area even if the plants are abundant. Conservation always takes precedence over creativity, and you need to be careful about how you gather plants. Generally, you can take as many tree leaves as you need (they're going to fall off and decay by the billion anyway), and most roadside or field flowers are so abundant that you can pick a specimen without harming anything.

- Know the identity of your specimen. There are poisonous plants out there and you want to make certain that you are not picking one of them.

- If you are on private land or in someone's garden and you see a flower you simply must hammer, ask permission before you pick it. Usually people are so enamored with the craft of hammered art, they're generous in giving you what you ask for.

paper towels. A chopping board is lightweight, readily available, and easily carried around, indoors or out. If your hammered impression turns out too faint, remove one layer of paper towel and try again. It it's still too faint, remove the remaining paper towel. Hammering on just the hard wooden surface may force out more of the plant's pigments. On the other hand, if the impression looks too squishy, add more padding beneath the material you're hammering.

Because hammering makes a lot of noise, you might want to put the chopping board on top of something like a telephone book or a stack of newspapers to absorb some of the sound. You can't hammer directly onto a soft surface, though, because you need the contact between the metal hammer and a hard surface to make the impression.

COVER MATERIALS

*B*esides having absorbent material under your chosen fabric or paper, you must also cover the plant. For most plants, a paper towel works well, and the thicker and fluffier, the better. Cheap paper towels absorb very little, meaning you simply need more of them, so you'll end up spending about the same on a large quantity of cheap paper towels that you would have spent on a smaller quantity of more expensive towels. A good alternative is to cover the plant with plastic (such as a piece of plastic wrap or a small plastic bag), which has the advantage of allowing you to see what you're doing. But the plastic has less absorbency than paper towels, so you might have to switch to using paper towels if your impression is not crisp.

Two other drawbacks to using plastic are that the plant material slips easily underneath the plastic, and it's difficult to determine if you have thoroughly hammered the plant. When you use a paper towel, the towel will absorb the pigments from the plant as you hammer and you can easily tell if you have thoroughly hammered the entire surface. If you use plastic, there's less absorption so you must check under the plastic as you work to make sure you have a good transfer.

Another possibility is to use tape as a cover material. Unless you tape over the entire plant surface, though, you must still use another cover material so the hammer won't pick up pieces of leaf or petal and deposit them somewhere you don't want them. If you decide to use tape when hammering onto paper, be sure you use the kind that is removable.

You can also use fabric as a cover for—or underneath—plant material. However, it is critical that for each image you hammer, the cover and bottom materials be perfectly clean. If you can wash and dry your cloth often enough, cloth is certainly a viable (and earth friendly) alternative, though throwaway paper towels are faster and easier.

MATERIALS CHECKLIST

In addition to the plant materials, fabric or paper, hammer, and "sandwiching" materials, you should have these craft supplies available to help you:

- Iron , clothes dryer, or oven for heat-setting the design
- Tweezers or wooden skewers for manipulating delicate plant material on fabric
- Brushes or feathers for brushing hammered plant material off the fabric
- Scotch tape—removable and double sided
- Plastic bags for storing mordanted fabrics
- Glue, fusible webbing, spray adhesive
- Straightedge or ruler
- Cutting mats
- Scissors
- Sewing machine
- Ribbons, trim, natural treasures (such as twigs, lichen, or dried flowers)
- Raffia, natural or colored
- Colored papers
- Tracing paper

Making Sample Cards

Having your own sample book allows you to flip through and see at a glance the different kinds of images you can get and which ones you want to use for your own projects. Another great advantage to having your own book of samples is that you can always make iron-on transfers or color paper copies from these samples, giving you ample material for dozens of different crafts (see page 29 for more details).

Here's how to make a book of sample cards:

1. Mordant one yard each of wool, cotton, silk, and linen. Refer to pages 23–24 for instructions on how to mordant fabric.

2. Cut the the fabrics into 3½ x 5 inch rectangles. For each plant or blossom that you experiment with, make impressions on the four different fabrics. If you prefer to work on paper rather than fabric, make your impressions on a variety of papers.

3. Attach each sample to an index card. On the back of the card, write down as much information as you think necessary. Include the date, the type of flower or plant, and the type of material on which the sample was hammered. You might even want to include information such as the specific bolt number of the fabric, where you purchased it, and how much it cost, in case you love the images produced and you want to do a large project using that specific type of fabric.

4. If you want to test the lightfastness of any image, make two sample cards using the same plant material and fabric. Place one card in a book, where it receives no light, and place the other one in a sunny window. Leave the cards untouched for anywhere from several days to a couple of weeks, then compare the cards.

5. If you want to test the washability of a particular sample, again make two samples using the same plant material and fabric. Wash one and leave the other unwashed. Then compare the cards.

6. Punch a hole in one end of each card and place the cards in a small binder. Now you have a sample book, similar to a fabric swatch book found at decorator fabric stores.

> *Sample cards allow you to compare, at a glance, the same plant on different fabrics. Each plant in the book was tested on cotton, silk, wool, and linen. Shown here from top are: impatiens, coleus, cosmos, and Japanese maple.*

Get
Set

PRETREATING FABRICS • HAMMERING TECHNIQUES
USING COVER MATERIALS • SETTING THE DESIGN • DUPLICATING THE IMAGES
ENHANCING THE IMAGES • CREATING A PLEASING DESIGN
CARING FOR FABRIC PROJECTS • BEYOND PAPER AND FABRIC

Techniques

Although the basic techniques for hammering flowers are very simple, you must keep in mind that you are working with live plant material, and no two plants are exactly alike. Variables—such as the age of the plants, the amount of moisture and pigment they contain, and how these react with various fabrics and papers—sometimes result in images that have to be thrown away, but they are also responsible for making each image unique. In this chapter I share my tricks of the trade, so you will learn how to deal with these variables and increase your success rate for making beautiful, lasting impressions.

Pretreating Fabrics

You can certainly hammer an instant image on a piece of fabric without doing anything to the cloth. But if you are going to use the fabric for a project, you will want to pretreat it with a mordant so that your images are true to the color of the plant and the pigments last as long as possible. Remember that a mordant is a substance used by dyers to cause cloth or yarn to

< Ferns and maple leaves make beautiful impressions for a variety of crafts, including decorating silk ribbon (upper left), for example.

more readily absorb pigments. Hammering artists use mordants for similar purposes, because cloth pretreated with a mordant tends to hold the color of the images longer. I pretreat my fabrics in an alum bath.

ALUM BATH

Although alum is the least caustic of all mordants, it's important to treat it with respect. Handle all mordants, including alum, as little as possible, wear rubber gloves, and never use the same equipment for cooking that you use for mordanting. See "Mordanting Equipment" on page 13 for more information.

Before you treat any fabric with alum, you must first wash it thoroughly, either by hand or in the washing machine. Wool, silk, and linen should be hand washed. Do not add fabric softener. Unless you have a very large vat or pan for mordanting, work with small lengths of cloth (1 yard or less) at a time to avoid wrinkling and to allow the mordant to be absorbed evenly. While the cloth is still wet, make an alum bath.

Making an Alum Bath

For 1 yard of cotton, linen, or wool or 1 to 1½ yards of thin silk, use:

4 tablespoons of alum
3 tablespoons of cream of tartar
20-24 cups of water

1. Mix the alum with 10 cups of warm water and pour into a large, flat nonreactive pan (enamel or stainless steel). Mix the cream of tartar in 10 cups of warm water and add to the alum solution. You can add a few more cups of water if your pan is large enough.

2. Add the wet cloth, carefully arranging so that it does not wrinkle. Put the pan on the stove and heat slowly to about 82°F (low) and simmer for 30 to 40 minutes. Move the fabric around in the pan during this time so the cloth takes up the mordant evenly. Leave the cloth in the mordant bath until it cools, then remove and rinse thoroughly. Dispose of the alum bath safely by pouring it on the ground outdoors, away from areas where pets and children play. Only use the alum bath once. (See page 13 for more information on handling alum safely.)

3. Dry the cloth, either by hanging it on a clothesline or putting it in the dryer. Do not use dryer sheets. The dryer is suitable for cotton, but other fabrics should be line dried to avoid wrinkling.

4. Iron the cloth and store by hanging it over a plastic or wooden hanger in a dark closet. Mark the type of cloth and the kind of mordant you used. It's now ready for pounding.

Hammering Techniques

Before you take hammer to fabric, be certain that there are no wrinkles in the material. It is better to iron the cloth before you hammer rather than after the image is on the fabric because the image itself may burn with a hot iron faster than the unadorned fabric.

The hammering surface is important. If the surface is too hard, the plant material may splatter and not give a crisp image. If it is too soft, it may be difficult to extract the pigments from the plant. A good starting point is to place the fabric on a wooden chopping board covered with a double layer of paper towels. Put your plant pieces on top of the fabric, and cover with another layer of paper towels. You are essentially sandwiching the fabric and plant pieces between materials that absorb excess moisture. (See "Cover Materials" on pages 17 and 27–28 for a discussion of various "sandwich" materials.)

Before you begin hammering, double check to make sure the plants are exactly where you want

Take your hammering materials and cloth out to the garden and have fun experimenting.

them to be. Once they are hammered, there is no erasing. And watch out for dirt, bugs, and little worms (I'm not kidding!). Flowers brought in from the garden often have a few "hitchhikers" and you don't want a squished bug in the center of your beautiful floral impression!

Begin by hammering gently, increasing the pressure as the image begins to transfer. A sudden blow to an unsuspecting leaf might result in pigments squirting out all over the place, so begin slowly and gently. This is particularly important when hammering thick parts, such as stems and flower centers. Once you have tapped down on a thick part, you can usually hammer with increasing pressure until you get a good transfer. Hammer as hard as the fabric and plant will take.

If you find that the pigments are not coming through very well, you can try hammering harder, taking away some of the padding underneath, or using plastic wrap or wax paper instead of a paper towel as cover material. Working with less

- Do read the information on individual flowers in the Plant Guide (pages 154–74), before you begin making impressions for projects.

- Do hammer petals, leaves, etc. in a single layer. Multiple layers produce a puddle of muddy colors.

- Do test and practice on your fabric before you begin a project.

- Do place the side with the most interest (color, venation, pattern, etc.) face down on your material to be hammered. If you don't like the results from one side, get another leaf or petal and try it with the opposite side down.

- Don't hammer wet plant material. If it has rained recently (or if you just watered the garden) take a paper towel and gently press on the plant until all moisture has been absorbed.

- Don't give up too quickly when you're trying out a new plant. Try working with varying thicknesses of paper towels to try to get a good transfer.

Left: muscadine hammered vein down
Right: muscadine hammered vein up

absorbency will help force the pigments onto the cloth. Sometimes, though, you'll find that some plants just give up their image readily.

On the other hand, if you find that the plant is splattering out all over the material, try adding more absorbency—another layer of paper towel on top, for example. If you're still not getting the image you want, try a different, more absorbent fabric (such as cotton flannel) or put the plant material in a book or plant press for a couple of hours before you hammer. This gets rid of some of the moisture and allows for a cleaner transfer. Timing is critical if you press the plant material first. If you leave it too long it might lose too much moisture and cannot be hammered. If you don't leave it long enough, you'll run into the same squishy problem.

Using Cover Materials

You might prefer to use plastic wrap as a cover material instead of paper towels whenever possible for the simple reason that you can see what you're doing. If you use plastic, be careful that the plant doesn't slip as you hammer it and be sure that you have hammered over the entire plant evenly.

You can also try using Scotch tape to secure the plant material to the fabric. It is more time consuming to make impressions this way, but tape is a wonderful tool because it keeps the plant from shifting while you hammer, resulting in a cleaner and crisper transfer. Using tape also makes it easier for young children and older adults to enjoy this craft because they don't have to struggle with using a hammer with one hand while securing plant material with the other.

Tape is also useful when you are making an impression that contains several separate plant pieces, such as when you are hammering 8 to 10 petals to "create" a chrysanthemum blossom. (If you do not use tape and you are working with several petals, try positioning and hammering them one at a time to be certain that your design is symmetrical.) You will still need an additional cover material unless the tape covers all of the plant. This is

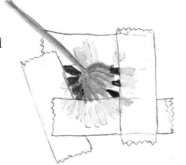

because the hammer picks up bits of plant and as you continue to hammer, you'll end up with surprise polka dots of color in the least expected places.

For really soft plants or flimsy fabric, tape is not effective

because you need the absorbency of the paper towel directly over the plant material.

After you have finished hammering, carefully lift the fabric and look at the underside before you remove the plant material. The bottom side will usually show any places you've missed with the hammer. If you have missed some spots, put the fabric back down (carefully!) and hammer again over those spots. Check the bottom side again and when it looks as if you have a thoroughly hammered design, remove the cover material and the hammered plant material.

If you get a great image on the cover material

- Be sure your fabric has no wrinkles before you hammer.

- Use a wooden chopping board covered with a double layer of paper towel. Put your project fabric or paper over this and position the plants exactly where you want them.

- Check for bugs and dirt.

- Put another paper towel over the plants and hammer gently but thoroughly.

- Readjust the absorbency level, if necessary, by adding or taking away paper towels.

- When you think you're done, check the underside of the project fabric or paper to see if you've missed any spots. Rehammer, if necessary.

- Remove cover material and plant pieces, taking care not to smear the fabric as you brush away the bits of plant.

as well as your project fabric, try making a "double image." Use a project fabric as a cover and see if you can't get two useful images with a single hammering. Be aware, though, that two pieces of fabric might be so absorbent that you end up with two vague images. Experiment a little before you hammer your project fabric or paper.

Be careful when you brush away the bits of plant from your fabric—the pigments are still wet and will smear easily. If the leaf or petal is firmly

embedded, allow it to dry thoroughly (an iron speeds this process), then gently scrape it off with a craft knife. You can use a feather to brush away plant pieces, or the sticky side of a piece of tape to clean up any loose odds and ends.

Setting the Design

After you have transferred your image, it is a good idea to set the transfer with heat to help keep the image from fading. For most impressions, the best way to do this is with a warm iron. If you are working with a very large piece of decorated fabric, you can use a warm (200°F) oven or a clothes dryer, though keep in mind that some fabrics dry better this way than others. For example, cotton is fine for the dryer but linen wrinkles too badly and should be heat-set with an iron.

If you decide to use an oven, be careful not to scorch the fabric or the design. Place foil on a large cookie sheet, lay the fabric flat on top of this, and cover with another piece of foil. Remember, the goal here is to set the design, not "brown in the oven." Wool, in particular, is sensitive to scorching in an oven. For any fabric, an iron is probably the easiest way to set the design to produce good results.

No matter what fabric you are working with, set the iron temperature at the appropriate setting for that fabric and iron thoroughly and firmly. Keep the iron on each part of the image for 45 to 60 seconds. Be very careful not to scorch the fabric.

The best way to set the design is to take it to a dry cleaners and have it pressed professionally.

Duplicating the Images

Modern technology offers machines, such as scanners and color copiers, that open up countless possibilities for using hammered art. The images you create by hammering flowers and leaves can be copied onto paper, cloth, or iron-on transfers (a special paper on which the image is printed and can then be ironed onto cloth). The advantages to using iron-on transfers, rather than hammering directly onto fabric, are that the images can then be worn in the sunshine and washed without fading. (another benefit if you're decorating clothing).

PAPER IMAGES

Although you can easily take your beautiful images to a copy service shop to be copied to paper or iron-on transfers, the equipment to make copies is not terribly expensive and you may find that you enjoy creating them at home.

With a scanner (which can be purchased for a little over $100) or a digital camera, a home computer, and a color printer, you can just about set up your own design business. However, professionally done copies are usually brighter and more vivid than ones made at home.

Once you have a hammered image that you like, put it into the scanner (or photograph it with a digital camera), send it to the computer, and you have that image (which won't fade!) stored for as long as you want or need it.

The same image can then be used as an appliqué for bags or clothing, to make note cards, decorate sheets and pillows, make birthday cards—the only limit is your imagination.

When you scan a hammered image, the scanner picks up the weave of the cloth as well as the image itself, causing gray areas in your copy.

Flower fairies can be created by hammering leaves and petals in different configurations.

You can partially solve this problem by placing the fabric in the scanner in such a way that it picks up the weave as little as possible. If your image shows a lot of gray and shadow, try turning the image in the scanner 90 degrees so the cloth faces a different direction and see if this doesn't help. You can also ease the problem by using a closely woven fabric so the individual threads do not show.

Once you have the image scanned into the computer, you can save it as a file or send it to the printer. When you print the image, be sure that you change the printer properties to accept the right kind of paper (iron-on transfer may be referred to as "special paper" in your print program). For best results, feed the paper through the printer one page at a time.

COPY PAPER

No matter how you are going to duplicate your image (on glossy paper, printable fabric, or iron-on transfers) you'll want to make the most of your copy paper, because all of these papers are expensive (at least $1 per sheet). If you are going to cut out your images to remount in different ways, place as many images on a page as possible, taping them to a sheet of 8½ x 11-inch paper, leaving a ½-inch margin around the edges of the paper. This duplicating method is particularly effective with iron-on

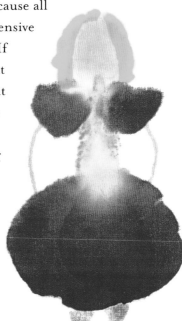

Once you have a sheet of good images, you can duplicate it as often as you like to make a multitude of crafts.

transfers because you will cut these out of the paper and trim close to the image itself anyway, so you need little margin between images. If you are duplicating an image to glossy paper that will be folded into a card, you'll have to limit yourself to a single image per sheet.

Iron-on transfer paper is available at office-supply stores and at craft stores. There are two types of transfer paper—one made for a color copy machine and another made for a color ink-jet printer. Be sure you choose the correct paper for your machine. One word of caution: Although manufacturers claim that the iron-on transfer paper goes through a variety of color copy machines, my experience has been different. I took the paper to two different copy services and tried the paper in machines recom-

mended by the transfer paper manufacturer. Both times the paper began to melt during the process. Although technology is certain to fix the problem in the near future, run a test sheet through the machine to be certain that the copy machine can successfully take the paper before you begin.

FABRIC IMAGES

It's possible to run some types of fabric through home printers as well. These fabric images are relatively lightfast but are not waterproof, meaning they cannot be washed (but can be dry cleaned). You can purchase special canvas that is designed to go through the printer (it costs about $1 a "page") or you can iron freezer paper to a thin cloth, which makes it stiff enough to go

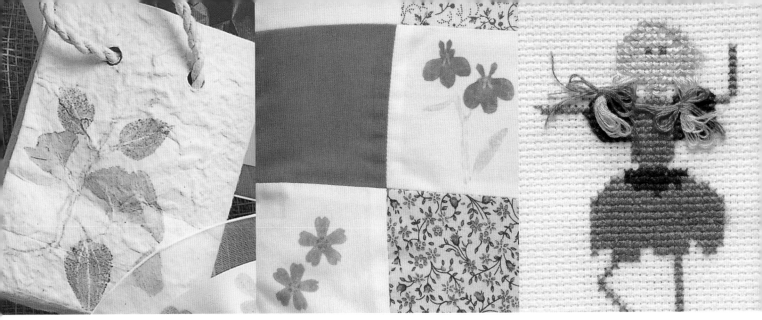

There's no end to the possibilities for using hammered images—from making gift bags to pillows to counted cross-stitch.

PRINTED POSSIBILITIES

The ability to print directly onto fabric is exciting in its potential. Although not all fabrics will go through the printer (linens and silks seem to do best) you can use the printed fabrics for a number of projects including:

- Printing your own cross-stitch or needlepoint designs (print directly on the cross-stitch fabric)

- Printing a hammered image on a piece of silk to use as a pillow front

- Printing an image to be used as the front of a gift bag

- Printing images to be used in quilts

- Printing an image on lightly patterned or colored fabric

- Printing an image on fabric you've hand dyed to make a truly unique project

through the printer (at a fraction of the cost).

Choose a lightweight linen, silk, or cotton and cut a piece of freezer paper about 9 x 12 inches. Iron the fabric to get all the wrinkles out, then iron the shiny side of the freezer paper to the back side of the fabric until all the edges are sealed and there are no bubbles. Then cut the melded fabric and paper to exactly 8½ x 11 inches, leaving no rough edges or strings from the fabric. Set the printer properties to "special paper" and feed into the printer one page at a time.

There are also commercially available fabric kits that contain silks that have been treated to make the ink from printers washable when they are steam set. You may want to try using one of these kits.

Enhancing the Images

The ephemeral quality of hammered art makes it special and exciting but it is frustrating to spend a lot of time and energy on a piece only to have it fade. There are ways, however, to capture more permanently the delicate, detailed beauty of the piece. The first is to enhance the image with paint; the second is to secure it with colored threads, as in cross-stitch, embroidery, or needlepoint. Both methods take considerably more time than simply hammering an image, but both result in lasting pieces.

PAINTING

Whether you are creating a piece of art to hang on the wall or simply securing a design on a sweatshirt so you can throw it into the washing machine, painting over your images has the same benefits—it protects the beauty of the piece from fading due to light and/or moisture.

Even if you think you can't paint, even if you haven't held a paintbrush since third grade, you can do this. If you are enhancing a design hammered onto fabric, use either fabric or acrylic paints. It's sometimes tricky to paint on fabric because the paint tends to run once it gets into the weave of the cloth, but hammering the plants into the fabric gives you an automatic surface that holds the paints better than raw fabric. You'll see this when you "paint outside the lines." If you've never painted on fabric before,

practice before you begin—but practice on a hammered image so you'll get the feel for painting on the same surface. You can add as much detail as you like; you have the guidelines right in front of you from the hammered image. It's just like painting by number!

If you are enhancing a piece of clothing that will go into the washing machine, use fabric paints. Check the paint label to determine its washability.

Bee balm on cross-stitch fabric.

CROSS-STITCH, NEEDLEPOINT, AND EMBROIDERY

Hammered images allow you to become your own designer, particularly when you create your own needlework patterns. If threads and yarns are more fun for you than paintbrushes, then by all means sew your designs instead. Hammered images can be transferred to canvas or linen for needlework in three ways: (1) hammered directly onto the fabric, (2) copied onto an iron-on transfer and then put on the fabric, or (3) scanned into the computer, then printed directly onto the fabric. Each method is viable, though printing the image directly onto the fabric to be sewn results in the most precise transfer. And although the colors and patterns are there and can be easily sewn, an accomplished needleworker can still find plenty of room for his or her own creative touches.

Creating a Pleasing Design

Although a single hammered image is beautiful, as you work more with this craft you'll want to put several images together to create a design. This is especially true when you're making your own decorative items, such as pillow shams, lampshades, or accent pillows. Arranging floral images on fabric is not too different from arranging flowers in a vase. In both cases, your goal is to combine colors and lines that are pleasing to the eye. Knowing a few basic elements of design will enable you to make your images blend and complement one another.

FOCAL POINT

A focal point draws the eye into the design and is the element that stands out the most. When working to fit multiple hammered images into a single design, you could choose a flower that is particularly large or bright, such as cosmos, as a focal point, or one that has intricate details, such as Queen Anne's lace. A grouping or cluster of plants could also serve as a focal point. Be careful that you don't include a "blooper" that would, by mistake, turn out to be your focal point.

STYLE

When creating a design, choose a single style. Just as there are different styles of flower arrangements (a bunch of daisies stuck in a mason jar is decidedly casual while a huge symmetrical

arrangement in your grandmother's crystal bowl is formal), there are also different styles of design to choose from when arranging floral impressions: formal or informal, cute or dignified, sophisticated or casual. Limit a single design to a single style. For example, if you've hammered a stunning chrysanthemum in one corner, creating an elegant and sophisticated look, you wouldn't want to add a row of cute "floral ballerinas" across the top. Determine the style of your design and work everything toward this end. When I designed the bedroom set (see pages 56–58), I wanted it to look light and casual, like flowers in a field, so I left plenty of space between the images and didn't try to make them even and symmetrical.

Here are some design rules to keep in mind:
Group like things. If, for example, you're working to fit images of vinca, Queen Anne's lace, and pansies into a single design, group the same kind of flowers together so that you have a cluster (or several clusters) of each, then use leaves to hold the design together. Groups of flowers read visually as a single element. The eye rests on these groupings, pausing to examine the individual components, then moves on to the next group. If you sprinkle single flowers all over the page, the eye jumps around trying to follow the images. Be easy on the eyes.

Use patterns and repetition. A pattern is the same

Arrange a hammered image to create a pleasing design.

image or sequence of images that appears at regular intervals. For example, you can easily make a beautiful border by alternating vinca blossoms with wisteria leaves, keeping the same amount of space between each image. It doesn't matter if you include two blossoms and two leaves or 50 of each; as long as they are the same image (or very close) and appear at regular intervals, you have a pattern. Patterns are easy and effective for many craft projects. Try putting a floral pattern across a sheet of paper, for example, and suddenly you have stationery! Repeating an image adds rhythm and texture and helps pull various elements of a design together. Repeated images need not be identical, but to create rhythm, should share some common feature—color, shape, or size. Just

don't overdo it, or the repetition will become boring rather than exciting.

Pay attention to what's NOT there as well as what's there. Called "negative spaces," these are blank areas on the canvas (or paper, fabric, etc.) created by the edges of the images. Negative spaces are particularly important when you are hammering clusters of flowers. If you hammer each blossom or floret too close to an adjacent one, it appears as a blob rather than two distinct and intricate flowers. Spaces between the individual flowers of a cluster are just as important as the flowers themselves. The same holds true for putting a number of flowers in a single design. If the images are too close together, the eye will read them as a single mass. When you are hammering flowers and leaves directly onto fabric (rather than using iron-on transfers) remember that the plant parts will spread slightly as you hammer them. Be certain to leave extra room between the parts. Remember, spaces are beautiful, too.

Keep it balanced. A strong design includes elements that balance each other, resulting in a sense of visual satisfaction. Size and color can both be used to balance a design. If, for example, you have three huge, bright pink cosmos blossoms in the bottom right-hand corner and a little Johnny-jump-up sitting by itself in the top left-hand corner, your design is going to slide right off the bottom of the page. To strengthen the design, you could put two dozen little Johnnys together on the top left to balance the cosmos and your design would be more balanced—a little unusual, but definitely more balanced!

IN A NUTSHELL

- Give the eye a place to start by including a focal point.

- Limit a design to a single style.

- Group like images—be easy on the eyes.

- Use pattern and repetition in your design to create rhythm and texture.

- Pay attention to what's not there—spaces are beautiful.

- Create visual satisfaction—keep it balanced.

Caring for Fabric Projects

Once you've created your first piece of hammered art, you'll want to be sure to take care of it so you can enjoy it for many seasons to come. I have only two rules for fabric care. My first is this: Don't wash any hammered art in liquids! Moisture makes the colors fade and liquids soak into the weave of the cloth or paper, releasing the crisp edges of the images, making them blurry. Although this might be used as a special effect, you'll want as clear and crisp a transfer as you can get. Fortunately, the images I've made—on all fabrics—dry cleaned beautifully.

Unless you have a garment or fabric that is specifically marked "Do Not Dry Clean," this remains the best method of caring for your projects. Not only does it help clean the fabric, it also helps heat-set the image. I often take new projects to the cleaners as soon as I finish them for this very reason.

My second rule: Protect your images from sunlight, which also makes the colors fade. Although a UV protective spray helps prevent fading to some degree, it's best not to expose any of the transfers to bright light.

I have tried every product imaginable in the hopes of finding something that would make hammered images water- and light-fast. I tried silk paint extender, (which didn't work on hammered images but is useful for printed designs, snow seal (well, it keeps nylon water-proof, doesn't it?), appliqué protectors (which took the color out immediately), decoupage glue (which took the color out after several hours), and many other products that did not work.

I found that live plant pigments react chemically with many products, resulting in an alteration in, or even loss of, color.

So, a word to the wise—be careful what you put on your images. Dry cleaning seems to be safe and UV spray will help protect the pigments from fading in the light. But all plants are different and react differently to chemicals, light, and heat. Before you spray, paint, cover, dip, or rub your images with anything, test it first.

Beyond Paper and Fabric: Working with Polymer Clay

The choice of surfaces to use for hammering impressions is fairly limited, but there are many fun and creative projects you can do by embedding flowers and leaves into polymer clay. This clay comes under many trade names including Sculpey, Fimo, and Cernit. Polymer clay is malleable and easy to work with, and stays soft until baked in the oven.

Unlike making impressions on paper or fabric, when making impressions in clay, you leave the plant parts in to become part of the design. You don't actually hammer the flowers into the clay as much as you gently push them in, though a hammer is often the best tool to

accomplish this. Flower petals and leaves often change colors when baked, so you'll need to test your particular plants before making items for a finished project.

After baking the clay, protect the piece by painting it with a glaze made specifically for polymer clay. But, again, be warned. Not only does the heat from baking change some plant colors, chemicals in the glaze often react with plant parts as well, causing colors to fade or change. For example, yellow coreopsis came out of the oven still yellow, but when painted with the glaze, it turned bright orange. Even though the glaze makes some flowers unsuitable for this craft,

Flowers and leaves react differently when baked into polymer clay. Coleus (far left) and leucanthemum (center) kept their color, while vinca (far right) turned brown.

it is important to cover the finished piece with the coating to secure the plant parts to the clay.

The following list offers a few examples of plants and how they reacted to heat and glaze on polymer clay:

* *All pink flowers tested (vinca, verbena, zinnia, etc.):* turned brown
* *Bright yellow lantana:* turned brown
* *Butter daisy (leucanthemum):* stayed yellow
* *Coleus:* turned a little brown but kept good color
* *Coreopsis:* turned bright orange
* *Grape leaf (green):* turned a mustard brown
* *Greens (most leaves, ferns):* stayed green
* *Lobelia:* blue turned a little darker but a beautiful result
* *Yellow black-eyed Susan:* stayed yellow
* *Zinnia (bright orange):* stayed orange

CLAY TIPS

Keep these guidelines in mind as you work with polymer clay:

- Be certain that you keep your work area as clean as possible, removing all bits and pieces of plants that could be inadvertently taken up by the clay.

- If you want to string medallions for a mobile or jewelry, put a small hole in the clay before you bake it.

- You can mold the clay into any shape—squares (for tiles) rounds, ovals—anything that suits your imagination and creativity.

- The thicker the pieces, the longer they should bake.

- Be sure to use separate utensils for working with clay—never use the same utensils for cooking.

Go!

EASY-TO-MAKE PROJECTS:
HOME DÉCOR • WEARABLE ART
GIFTS AND ACCESSORIES • CELEBRATION WARE

Home Décor

Botanic images can be easily incorporated into almost any home decorating scheme, and there are numerous items you can create to enhance your living space—from floral images on fabrics to framed fern prints. Even if your technical skills don't extend beyond a hammer, you can still make beautiful impressions for pillows, wall art, lamp shades, and table linens. Choose from among these exciting projects:

PINK DOGWOOD TABLECLOTH AND NAPKINS

CABBAGES AND KINGS PILLOW

VIOLA SLEEP PILLOW

QUILT SQUARE PILLOW

WISTERIA WALL QUILT

PILLOW SHAM

VALANCE

LAMP SHADE

FLOORCLOTH

AUTUMN COLLAGE

NAPKIN RINGS

PLACE MATS AND NAPKINS

FERN TEA TOWELS

FLORAL CLOCK

BALLET CLASS PICTURE

HERB TILES

FLOWER PRINTS

Pink Dogwood Tablecloth and Napkins

This tablecloth fits over a card table and, combined with the napkins, makes the perfect place setting for a spring luncheon. The dogwood has a graceful floral shape, and transfers a beautiful soft pink color. I hammered the original impression on a closely woven smooth cotton, had it copied onto iron-on transfer paper, and then put the design on a piece of heavy cotton.

⅓ yard of good-quality, closely woven, white cotton or linen
12-15 small pink dogwood blossoms
25-30 dogwood leaves
White cotton tablecloth, approximately 60 inches square
4 white cloth napkins
2 sheets of 8½ x 11-inch iron-on transfer paper
Hammer
Iron

1. Cut the piece of cotton or linen approximately 8½ x 11 inches.

2. Hammer the blossoms and leaves one at a time onto the piece of fabric. Place them as close together as you can and make sure that all your impressions fit within an 8½ x 11-inch sheet of paper.

3. Copy the hammered impressions onto iron-on transfer paper.

4. Wash and iron the tablecloth and napkins.

5. Cut all the blossoms and leaves out of the transfer paper, cutting as close to the image as possible.

6. Lay the tablecloth out flat. Place two to three iron-on blossoms and several leaves at each corner of the tablecloth and iron the transfers onto it.

7. Iron the remaining transfers onto the napkins, placing the images toward the bottom right-hand corner of each napkin.

~

Cost: $ Time: 2–4 hours Difficulty: easy–moderate

THE ART AND CRAFT OF POUNDING FLOWERS

Throw Pillows

*E*ach of these three pillows was made with a theme in mind. I made the Cabbages and Kings Pillow for my sister, who is a Lewis Carroll fan, and included a quote from the author along with cabbage leaf impressions. The small Viola Sleep Pillow has dried viola petals stuffed inside to ensure a restful night's sleep, while the Quilt Square Pillow showcases other early spring blooms.

Cabbages and Kings Pillow

*T*he quote on this pillow reads: *The time has come, the walrus said, to talk of many things: of shoes, and ships, and sealing wax, of cabbages and kings, of why the sea is boiling hot, and whether pigs have wings.*

When I tried hammering the beautifully-veined flowering cabbage leaf, I found that the leaf had too much moisture in it to transfer well. So I pressed it in a book to dry overnight and got a better impression the next morning.

These same images can be hammered onto a closely woven cotton and you can use the fabric to make kitchen curtains or chair cushions.

Flowering cabbage leaves
Plant press or heavy book
Paper towels
⅓ yard of mordanted fabric (I used white cotton flannel.)
Fabric pen
1½ yards of ¼-inch purple satin ribbon for bows
Craft glue
Sewing machine or needle and thread
Polyester stuffing or fiberfill
Hammer
Iron
Scissors

1. Pick several leaves off an ornamental cabbage plant and place them in a plant press or a heavy book. If using a book, place the leaves between pieces of paper towel before putting them into the book. Allow them to dry overnight or for several hours. Do not press them longer than 10-12 hours, or they will lose too much moisture.

2. Test a leaf on a scrap piece of fabric. If it is still too juicy, press another couple of hours. When you hammer, you can alter the absorbency of the fabric as needed by changing the thickness of the paper towel padding above and below the fabric to get the best possible transfer.

3. Cut two pieces of mor- danted fabric approximately 12 x 16 inches, and iron the fabric.

4. Position the cabbage leaves and hammer them onto the fabric. Heat-set the images with the iron.

5. Use the fabric pen to write the quote on the fabric. If desired, you can type this on a computer in an italic font, then print it on iron-on transfer paper (be sure to hit the "mirror image" key so you can read the words). Then you can simply iron on the letter- ing. You can type the quote as a paragraph and position the leaves around it as a frame.

6. Make small bows and glue or sew them onto the front of the pillow as desired.

7. Place the two pillow pieces right sides together. Stitch along three sides, using a ½-inch seam.

8. Turn the pillowcase right side out and gently stuff with the polyester. Use small, hidden stitches to sew up the open side.

~

COST: $ TIME: 1–2 hours   DIFFICULTY: moderate

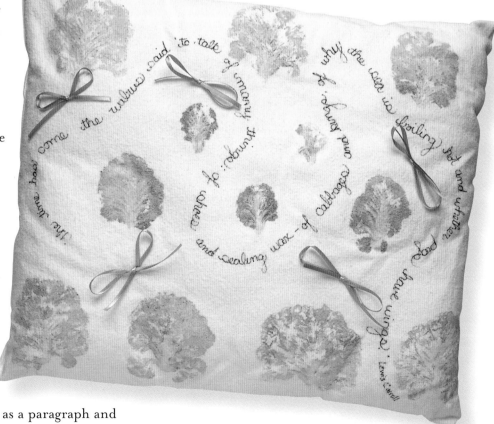

Viola Sleep Pillow

This charming pillow is great for decorating a guest room bed or to give as a gift. Drawing from the traditions of aromatherapy (the use of scents to alter mood) and the Victorian belief in the language of flowers (which identified individual flowers with specific meanings, such as love, purity, faithfulness, and so on), sleep pillows are filled with herbs or flowers that are thought to inspire dreams. See "The Language of Flowers" at right for a list of flowers that can be used in sleep pillows.

¼ yard of white, mordanted fabric
¼ yard of white or other color fabric (doesn't have to be mordanted)
Pencil
Compass
Viola blossoms and leaves
¾ yard of ½-inch braid or trim to match blossom colors
¼ cup of dried viola petals or potpourri
Sewing machine or needle and
    thread
Polyester stuffing or fiberfill
Hammer
Iron
Scissors

1. Iron the mordanted fabric and use the pencil to mark off an 8 x 6½-inch rectangle.

2. Use the compass to make a 5-inch-diameter circle, centered within the rectangle.

THE LANGUAGE OF FLOWERS

Angelica: inspiring dreams

Baby's-breath: happy dreams

Cloves: vivid dreams

Everlasting: dreams of remembrance

Geranium: spiritual, calm dreams

Lavender: relaxing, loving dreams

Lemon balm: comforting dreams

Pansy: dreams of absent lovers

Periwinkle: dreams of sweet memories

Phlox: dreams of love

Pinks: dreams of affection

Rosemary: dreams of remembrance

Roses: dreams of love

Spearmint: relaxing dreams

Thyme: restful dreams

Yarrow: dreams of loved ones

3. Using the circle as a guide, position the viola blossoms and leaves into a wreath shape and hammer them onto the mordanted fabric. Heat-set the images with the iron.

4. Cut out the mordanted fabric rectangle. This is the pillow front. Sew braid to the front of the rectangle, ½ inch in from each side.

5. Cut an 8 x 6½-inch rectangle from the second piece of white fabric for the pillow back. Place the two pillow pieces right sides together and stitch around three sides, being careful not to catch the braid in the seam.

6. Turn the pillowcase right side out and stuff lightly with the polyester. Add the dried viola petals or potpourri and sew up the open side, using small, hidden stitches.

~

Cost: $ Time: less than 1 hour Difficulty: easy–moderate

Make It Simple: Hammer one or two large viola blossoms onto a small white pillowcase. Stuff with dried petals and a small pillow. Sew up the open side.

Quilt Square Pillow

This pillow isn't actually quilted. Instead, I hammered small spring blossoms onto fabric and copied the fabric onto a sheet of iron-on transfer paper. The same idea could be used to make a very nice wall hanging by increasing the number of squares and quilting through batting and backing.

This is a very simple pattern that is great for those who have always wanted to make a quilt but were nervous about starting. Just be sure to measure and cut carefully so that the seams and squares will be even.

¼ yard of white cotton fabric

Small pieces of calico and solid-colored cotton fabric to make 3-inch squares

    (Take your hammered images to the fabric store so you can match the colors.)

½ yard of calico (or solid color) for border and pillow back

Spring flowers—enough to make at least 8 images

1 sheet of iron-on transfer paper

Sewing machine or needle and thread

14-inch pillow form

Ruler

Hammer

Iron

Scissors

1. Wash and dry all fabrics. Do not use fabric softener or dryer sheets.

2. Hammer the spring flowers onto the white fabric. Make iron-on transfers from this.

3. Iron all of the fabrics and cut eight 3-inch squares out of the white fabric. Make sure the squares are exactly 3 inches on each side. Cut out the iron-on transfer images and iron one image to each white square, centering the image on the square.

4. Cut four 3-inch squares from the calico fabric and four 3-inch squares from the solid-colored fabrics, again making sure the squares are exact. Lay out the quilt squares, alternating the white squares with the solid-colored or the calico squares. You will have four rows of four squares each.

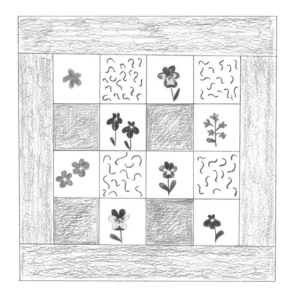

5. When you are pleased with your design, stitch the squares together, using a ¼-inch seam. To keep everything in the right order, stitch the first row, then the second, and so on. Iron all the seams open, then stitch the rows together, making sure that the corners of the squares meet. This is your pillow top.

6. Cut two strips of the border fabric 12 inches long and 1½ inches wide. Cut two more pieces 15 inches long and 1½ inches wide, or to match the width of the pillow top. It's a good idea to measure your pillow top before cutting the border pieces and adjust as necessary. Quilt squares have a nasty habit of changing sizes on you as you work with them!

7. Stitch the two 12-inch border pieces along the sides of the pillow top. Trim the ends even with the sides of the pillow top and iron open the seams.

8. Stitch the two 15-inch border pieces along the top and bottom of the pillow top, trim the ends, and iron open the seams. If you wish, you can add braid or other edging around the pillow top.

9. Cut a piece of calico for the backing, the same size as the front, including the borders. Place the two pillow pieces right sides together and stitch along three sides, leaving the bottom open.

10. Insert the pillow form and sew up the open side using small, hidden stitches.

~

Cost: $$ Time: about 2 hours Difficulty: moderate

Holiday Suggestion: Hammer asparagus fern to white squares, then create the pillow top by alternating the white squares with red squares for an attractive holiday accessory.

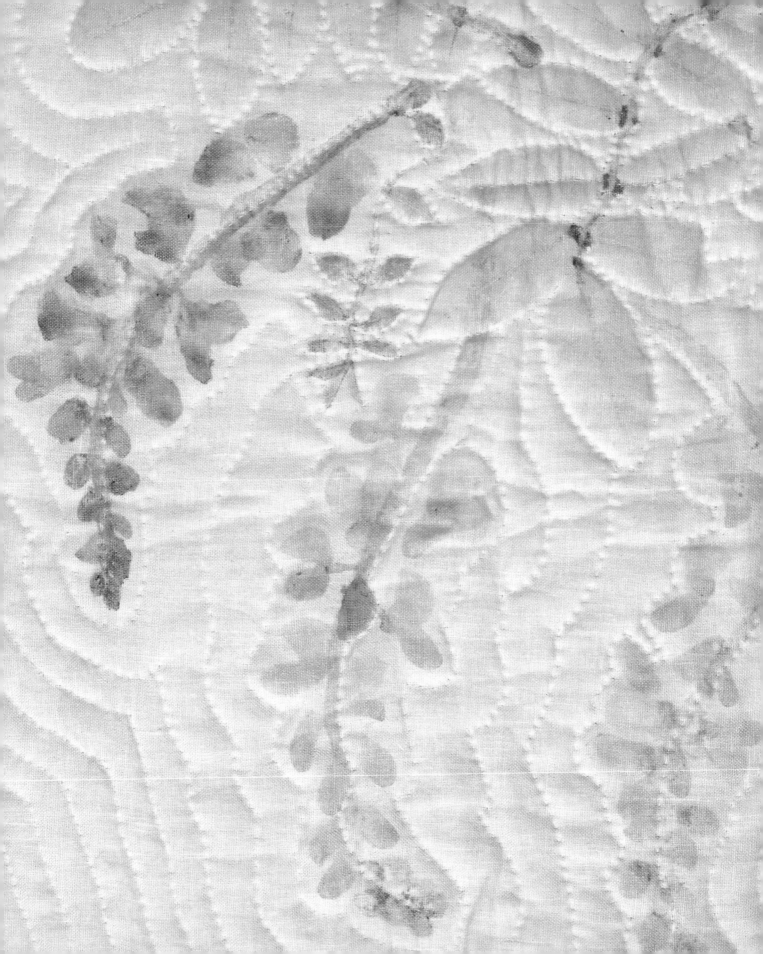

Wisteria Wall Quilt

This is truly an heirloom craft—a time-consuming labor of love that you will want to keep in the family for generations to come. But I think it's the prettiest craft in the book and well worth the effort. The quilting takes a long time, but it gives this wall hanging a 3-D look that makes it so appealing.

1 cluster of wisteria blossoms
Several dozen wisteria leaves, still attached to the stem
1¼ yards of white mordanted linen
1 small roll of quilt batting (crib size)
1¼ yards of white fabric for backing (linen or cotton)
Quilting needle and thread
Lap quilting hoop or small quilting frame
Hammer
Iron
Scissors

1. Iron the mordanted linen, then cut a piece 28 x 26 inches. Use a scrap of leftover linen to practice hammering wisteria blossoms and leaves. *Note:* Wisteria fades rapidly into subtle antique shades. Although the leaves look bright green at first, they will soon turn a golden color. If you want to speed up this process, place the hammered cloth in direct sunlight for several hours.

2. Position the blossom cluster, stem, and leaves on the fabric until you have a pleasing design, and hammer onto the fabric.

3. Turn the raw edges 1 inch toward the face of the quilt on all sides. Press. The quilt top should measure 26 x 24 inches.

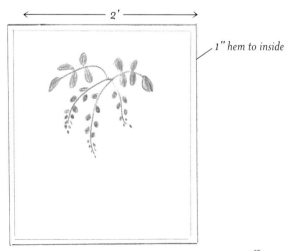

2'

1" hem to inside

4. To make the border, cut two pieces of treated white linen, 3½ inches wide by 28 inches long (includes a 1-inch hem) and two pieces 3½ inches wide by 24 inches long. Hammer the wisteria leaves to these strips of fabric in an overall pattern.

← 3½" →

5. Heat-set the images with the iron.

6. Hem the border strips by pressing under ½ inch along both lengths, making the pieces 2½ inches wide.

← 2½" → ½" hem

7. Take the two shorter border strips and place them at the top and bottom of the quilt top. Match the top edge of one border with the top edge of the quilt top. Pin or baste the edges together, then hand-stitch into place along the top and bottom of the border strip. Pin or baste the other short border piece at the bottom of the quilt and stitch in place. From top to bottom, the inside edges of the borders should be 21 inches apart.

stitch

19"

8. Make a 1-inch hem by pressing under the top and bottom raw edges of the long border pieces. Place these pieces along the side edges. Pin or baste, then hand-stitch the borders into place. From side to side, the inside edges of the borders should be 19 inches apart. The quilt top is now complete.

9. Cut the backing and quilting batting slightly larger than quilt top, leaving about a 2-inch margin on all sides. As you quilt, the top piece tends to stretch out a little and you want plenty of extra backing to adjust for this.

10. Place the backing on a clean table top. Place the batting over the backing, then place the quilt top on top of the batting. Smooth out the fabrics to make sure that each piece lies flat and the quilt top is centered.

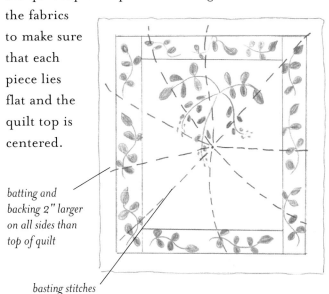

batting and backing 2" larger on all sides than top of quilt

basting stitches

VARIATIONS ON A THEME

Wisteria lends itself to this project because of its graceful form. However, you can make a wall quilt using any number of different plants. For example, if you want something more vibrant, try using bee balm or coreopsis. If you want a design with more detail, you might try using ferns.

11. Baste all three layers together. Start at the center and work your way out to each corner and edge. Include enough stitches so that the three pieces are held firmly together.

12. Using a quilting hoop or frame, quilt around the floral and leaf design, then continue this same basic quilting pattern toward the edges of the quilt, placing rows of quilting stitches about ½ inch apart until you reach the borders. The border can be quilted or left plain.

13. Trim the batting slightly smaller than the quilt top. Trim the backing so that it extends 1 inch past the quilt top on each side, then press this 1-inch hem toward the inside of the quilt, making the backing exactly the same size as the top.

14. Hand-stitch the outside edges together, then remove the basting stitches.

~

COST: $$ TIME: many, many hours DIFFICULTY: hard

quilt around design

hand stitch around edges

Bedroom Set

I used a combination of spring and summer flower images to decorate the guest room in my home. I used iron-on transfers for everything, because I wanted the images to last a long time without fading.

For most designs you might use a combination of flowers and leaves. I hammered a page of wisteria leaves and summer flowers (hollyhock, miniature bee balm, vinca, nigella, scabiosa, and an occasional petunia) for the projects that follow.

Pillow Sham

Use individual floral images to create a spray or bouquet of blossoms for a beautiful decorative pillow sham. The images can be hammered directly onto the pillow sham, but for long-lasting decorations, use iron-on transfers.

> Plain white pillow sham with decorative border, any size
> (I used a 20 x 26-inch sham, without the trim.)
> Iron-on transfers, created from hammered images
> Pencil
> Fabric marker or acrylic paints and paint brushes (for stem) or
> images of stems for transfers
> Iron
> 8½ x 11-inch paper

1. Place a clean, ironed pillow sham on a flat surface, right side up. (If you decide to hammer directly onto the cloth, treat it first with an alum bath.) Cut out the iron-on transfer images as precisely as possible, leaving little of the background paper.

2. Turn the images right side up so you can see the colors, but remember that you'll actually use them colored side down. Although you can create any design you like, the pillow shape lends itself to a symmetrical design. My design is a bouquet of flowers in a basic triangular shape, narrow at the base, wider at the top. Play with the images until you are pleased with the design.

When you are satisfied, take a pencil and mark on a piece of paper where each flower transfer is to go, and pencil in where you would like the stems to appear.

3. Mark the center of the pillow sham at the bottom edge. Leave a couple of inches for a bottom margin and begin your design at this point.

4. Iron each blossom and leaf transfer to the pillow sham at the designated place. (Or hammer the blossoms and leaves onto the pillow sham, if you are using that method.) If you find it difficult to iron the images through the double thickness of the pillow sham, try placing a hard surface, such as a small chopping board, inside the pillow sham so that you are ironing on only one thickness of fabric.

5. Use a fabric marker or paints to lightly paint in stems—don't overpower your design with heavy, bulky stems. If you are not comfortable using markers or brushes, you can always make iron-on transfers of stems to use instead. (Nandina stems are an excellent choice for this.)

~

Cost: $$$ Time: 1–2 hours Difficulty: moderate–hard

Make It Simple:
Use iron-on transfers of hammered images as a floral border for a pillowcase or pillow sham.

Valance

A single row of blossoms and leaves adds just the right touch to a plain white valance (or curtain). Since light coming in through the window will fade hammered images, use iron-on transfers instead of hammering the flowers directly onto the valance.

Plain white cotton valances (as many as you need for the room)
Iron-on transfers, created from hammered images
Pencil
Iron
Scissors

1. Iron the valances until all wrinkles are gone. Test an iron-on transfer on the back side of one valance to make sure it takes the image well.

2. Cut out the iron-on transfer images as precisely as possible, leaving little of the background paper.

3. Position the images in a pleasing pattern along the bottom of each valance. Be sure to leave a 1- or 2-inch margin at the bottom. Group two or three similar blossoms together, bordered on each side by a spray of leaves. Skip a small space and do another small grouping. If your images are all of the same blossom, you might want to simply line them up along the bottom of the valance.

4. When you are pleased with the design, use a pencil or pen to lightly mark on the valance where each image will go. Then move the transfers to a table, keeping them in the same order. Iron the transfers one at a time onto the valance in the designated places.

~

Cost: $$$ Time: less than 1 hour Difficulty: easy

Lamp Shade

This one-of-a-kind lamp shade is actually a breeze to make. That's because you start with a self-adhesive shade that you then cover with the fabric of your choice. These shades come in a variety of sizes and are covered with sticky paper to which fabric readily adheres. The sticky part is protected with a paper wrapper that you can use as a pattern to cut your fabric. If you cannot find this particular type of lamp shade, you can glue your decorated fabric onto a plain paper lampshade.

Self-adhesive lampshade
Plain white fabric (Each 7 x 12 x 8-inch shade requires ½ yard of fabric.)
Trim (Each 7 x 12 x 8-inch shade requires 1⅛ yards of trim.)
Craft glue
Iron-on transfers, created from hammered images
Iron
Scissors

1. Take the paper wrapper off the shade and use it as a pattern to cut the white fabric, adding a 1-inch margin all around the pattern.

2. Cut out the iron-on transfer images as precisely as possible, leaving little of the background paper.

3. Place the fabric on a flat surface and position the images in a pleasing pattern. Group several blossoms together, surrounded or bordered by leaves. Your shade will look more balanced if your images are positioned toward the bottom of the shade rather than around the center.

4. When you are pleased with your design, iron the images onto the fabric.

5. Place the fabric on the sticky side of the shade with 1-inch margins at the top and bottom and on the side where you will have a seam. Use your iron (on low) to press the fabric to the shade, smoothing out all wrinkles as you go. (The adhesive is fairly forgiving so you will be able to reposition the fabric as needed.) Work with the positioning until your images are straight and where you want them.

6. Trim the top, bottom, and side edge to a ⅜-inch seam (but no less).

7. Fold over the end of the fabric at the back seam and secure with craft glue.

8. Make small slits in the top edge of the fabric so it lies flat when turned to the inside. Turn both the top and bottom edges to the inside and secure with glue, rolling the fabric under for a smooth fit.

9. Glue the trim along the top and bottom edges and over the seam, if desired.

~

Cost: $$–$$$ Time: 1–2 hours Difficulty: moderate

VARIATIONS ON A THEME

You can use the iron-on transfers for a large variety of items, including wallpaper borders, pillow shams, valances, and lamp shades. But don't stop there—you can also decorate sheets and pillowcases, bedspread borders, curtains, and so on. I have even transferred small images to cross-stitch fabric to make a wonderful little wall hanging (see "Variations on a Theme" on page 75). For details on how to make iron-on images see pages 29–31.

Floorcloth

Painted heavy canvases made into area rugs are popularly known as floorcloths; try hammering leaves, flowers, and vines onto the canvas to create your own stunning piece of home décor. If you use a plant that fades quickly, or if you are using your floorcloth in an area that receives a lot of sun, you should consider enhancing it with paint before you cover the images with a protective sealant (see "Flower Prints" on pages 78–80 for details).

Heavy primed canvas made for floorcloths
Leaves, stems, and flowers
Acrylic paints (optional)
3¾ yards of upholstery trim
Hammer
Iron
Clear acrylic sealant

1. Cut the canvas to 36 x 24 inches (welcome mat-size). Put the canvas on the floor and lay the plants out in a pleasing design. Create a border, mirror images, or whatever you like. Vines are wonderful for making a graceful border design. I used kudzu for this floorcloth.

2. Sketch your design on a piece of paper, then remove the plant pieces from the canvas.

3. Replace a few plants at a time and hammer them onto the *unprimed* side of the canvas. This is very important. The primed side will not take an impression—the pigments slide right off. But the back side of a primed canvas takes the images much better than even an unprimed canvas does.

4. Continue hammering until your design is complete. Heat-set the images with the iron.

5. Enhance the images with paint, if desired, then hem or cover the raw edges of the canvas with upholstery trim.

6. If you have enhanced the images with paint, wait 24 hours until the pigments are completely dry, then seal the canvas with a clear acrylic sealant. Before you seal the entire piece, practice on a scrap to make sure the sealant does not make the hammered art fade.

~

COST: $$$ TIME: 3-4 hours DIFFICULTY: hard

Autumn Collage

As I watched the leaves falling off the Japanese maple in my backyard, I thought it would be fun to capture them in a collage to frame and display. I'd love to do four of these collages with hammered art—one for each season to hang as a grouping or to change as the seasons progress.

Pieces of dried grass, moss, twigs, pressed leaves, and raffia

Computer print, colored pencil, paint, or calligraphy pen for lettering

About 20 Japanese maple leaves, various sizes and colors, or 20 iron-on transfer images of leaves

Picture frame with 11 x 14-inch opening

14 x 16-inch bark paper or other textured paper (be sure it will accept either hammered images or iron-on transfers from the images)

14 x 16-inch foam board

UV protective spray

Craft glue and glue stick

Paper and pencil

Ruler

Hammer

Iron

Scissors

1. If you are going to use iron-on transfers, hammer the leaves onto closely woven fabric, then copy onto iron-on transfer paper. If you decide to hammer them directly onto the paper, practice on a test piece of paper first. I chose an unusual piece of bark paper for my project, which was beautiful, but the hammered impressions would not show up, so I had to use iron-on transfers. (I hammered 20 different leaves onto fabric, scanned the fabric into the computer, and printed it on iron-on transfer paper.)

2. Design the entire piece before you make anything permanent. Start by placing the leaves or the cut-out images randomly on the paper, in a graceful cascade starting at the top left-hand corner. Overlap them but leave plenty of interesting negative spaces (see "Creating a Pleasing Design" on pages 35–37).

3. Add woodland treasures to give the piece a 3-D look. (I included a real pressed maple leaf and a tiny bundle of dried wheat tied with raffia.) Position these in a pleasing way.

4. If you want lettering on your piece, include it as you work on your design. I wrote out the word "Autumn" in an airy, flourishing script, using colored pencils. When you are pleased with the overall design, take a piece of paper and carefully sketch out the entire design so that you can reassemble it back on the project paper. If you use iron-on transfer leaves, you can number them on the back to keep them in order.

5. Write, paint, draw, or copy any script onto the project paper at the desired spot. Don't forget that you can make an iron-on transfer of lettering as well as the leaves if you have a "mirror image" key on your computer.

6. Hammer or iron on the leaves in the designated places. Glue on any real treasures—grass, leaves, twigs, etc.

7. Spray with a UV protective spray.

8. Use glue to adhere the decorated piece to the foam board, then insert into the picture frame. I purchased an inexpensive wooden frame without glass, but you can also put this in a 3-D or shadowbox frame with glass, which is more expensive but protects the artwork better.

~

COST: $$ TIME: 2 hours DIFFICULTY: moderate–hard

Napkin Rings

Bright grosgrain ribbon and covered buttons decorated with small hammered flowers make unique napkin rings that will delight even the most discriminating dinner guest. These can be made in any color, using any small flower that matches your table setting. I chose blue ribbon and lobelia blossoms.

Plain wooden, plastic, or glass napkin rings (make sure they are no wider than your ribbon)

1-inch wide grosgrain ribbon, 16 inches long (more or less, depending on the size of the napkin rings)

½-inch diameter metal button forms (available at craft or fabric stores)

Scraps of mordanted white linen

Small blossoms that fit on the buttons

Glue

Needle and thread

Hammer

1. Cut approximately 10 inches of ribbon. Turn under both short ends to make tiny hems, or cut with pinking shears so the ribbon will not unravel.

2. Using a basting stitch, sew along one of the long edges. Be certain that the thread is secure at one end.

3. When you have sewn to the opposite end, gently pull the thread to gather the ribbon into a rosette. Make it as close and tight in the center as possible and stitch to secure. Set aside.

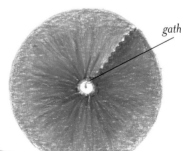

gather thread to make a rosette

cover button and sew to center of rosette

sew basting thread length of cut ribbon

4. Measure around the napkin ring and cut another piece of ribbon slightly longer than this measurement.

5. Glue the longer pieces of ribbon flat to the napkin ring, overlapping the edges.

6. To cover the buttons, measure the fabric according to the size indicated on the button packaging and cut the fabric covers.

7. Hammer a single image of a flower in the center of the cut fabric. (Be sure to cut extras, just in case you're not pleased with all the images you hammer.)

8. Use the decorated fabric to cover the button according to the manufacturer's directions, then sew the button to the center of the rosette.

9. Glue the rosette with button side up to the napkin ring, covering the lapped edges.

~

COST: $ TIME: about 15 minutes each DIFFICULTY: moderate

Place Mats and Napkins

*M*any summer flowers make beautiful, striking impressions. Among the best of these are bee balm, Queen Anne's lace, coleus, and cosmos, all of which I used to decorate a set of place mats and napkins. The images on the place mats were hammered directly onto the fabric, but those on the napkins were made from iron-on transfers so the napkins can be washed.

Place Mats

Flowers and leaves (I used bee balm, cosmos, Queen Anne's lace, and coleus.)

2 yards of heavy cotton twill or canvas fabric for place mats

4 ready-made white napkins, or 1 yard of lighter weight white fabric

7½ yards of trim for place mats

2 yards of iron-on vinyl

Sewing machine or needle and thread

Craft glue

1 sheet of iron-on transfer paper (for napkins)

Hammer

Iron

Scissors

1. Wash and mordant the heavy fabric. Iron out all the wrinkles.

2. Cut four 15 x 19-inch mats from the fabric (this includes a ½-inch hem on each side—the finished mats will measure 14 x 18 inches).

3. Hammer the flowers and leaves onto the place mats. Heat-set the images with the iron.

4. Using a sewing machine or needle and thread, sew a ½-inch hem all the way around each mat.

5. Cut a piece of iron-on vinyl to completely cover each mat and adhere the vinyl to the mat, following the manufacturer's directions.

6. Cut enough trim to go around all the edges of each place mat (about 64 inches per mat). Allow extra inches so you don't come up short when you cut it. Use craft glue to secure.

Napkins

1. Take smaller pieces of the same flowers you used for the place mats and hammer them onto the fabric of your choice to get good, clear impressions. Keep the impressions spaced apart a bit and make enough impressions for four napkin corners.

2. Make iron-on transfers from the images. Cut out the images as precisely as possible, leaving little of the background paper.

3. Position one transfer (color side down!) on the right-hand corner of a napkin and iron firmly, making sure to apply as much pressure as possible. Repeat for the remaining napkins.

~

Cost: $$ Time: several hours Difficulty: moderate

ABOUT IRON-ON TRANSFERS

Once you create a hammered image on fabric, you can duplicate it onto iron-on transfer paper, which then allows you to iron the image onto other fabrics. There are several advantages to using these iron-on images rather than freshly pounded ones:

- Iron-on images will last for many years indoors or outdoors without fading.

- Fabric with iron-on images can be washed without harming the images.

- If you have a favorite pounded image, you can make duplicate copies and have images to use for many projects.

If you have a computer, color printer, and scanner at home, you can easily make your own iron-on transfers. Or you can take your pounded images to a copy shop to be copied onto transfer paper. The basic procedure is to create hammered images on fabric and then have them copied onto transfer paper. You'll find detailed instructions for creating iron-on transfers on pages 29–31.

Fern Tea Towels

$\mathcal{O}$ne of the easiest ways to learn how to enhance hammered images with paint is to decorate a tea towel or hand towel. You can buy these inexpensive towels at craft or fabric stores.

3 small ferns or fern pieces
Tea towel with canvas border (designed for use with cross-stitch)
Green and brown fabric paints
Paintbrush
Hammer
Iron

1. Hammer the ferns onto the towel border. When you are through, be sure to remove all plant parts.

2. Mix acrylic paint to match the natural fern colors. Using the image as a pattern, paint, putting in as much or as little detail as you like. Don't paint too heavily, though—you want to still see the original image.

3. Allow the paint to dry thoroughly, then heat-set the images with the iron.

~

Cost: $ Time: less than 20 minutes Difficulty: easy—moderate

Floral Clock

Use small rounds of clay, hammered with bits of flowers and leaves, to decorate a wall clock. I chose small leaves and flowers that I knew would take the baking and glazing process, and the result is a real conversation piece.

Small flowers, leaves, and ferns (I used melampodia, New York fern, coleus,
   Queen Anne's lace, nandina leaves, thyme leaves and blossoms, zinnia, pink verbena,
   marigold, lantana, walking fern, muscadine leaves.)
Wooden clock base (Make sure it has enough flat space around the perimeter to hold
   the clay medallions.)
Wood stain
Clear varnish (optional)
About 4 ounces of polymer clay
Plastic wrap
Rolling pin
1½-inch round cookie or biscuit cutter
Glaze for clay
Small paintbrush
Foil-lined baking sheet
Oven
Clockworks and set of hands
Hot glue or craft glue
Press-on numerals (optional)

1. Stain the wooden clock base. Add a protective coat of varnish, if desired.

2. Roll out the clay on a large piece of plastic wrap to a thickness ⅛ to ¼ inch. Use the cookie cutter to make 12 clay medallions.

3. Place a small fern or flower in the center of each medallion. To make sure that your plant pieces remain attractive after baking and glazing, practice and try out several different plants before you decide on a final list. Even if the plants change colors slightly, they can still be appealing.

4. Place the medallions on the foil-lined sheet and bake at 275°F for 8–10 minutes until the clay has set.

5. Allow the medallions to cool, then use a small paintbrush to cover them with a protective coat of glaze.

6. Following the manufacturer's instructions, add the clockworks and hands to the clock base.

7. Glue the medallions to appropriate places on the clock face, representing the numbers 1 through 12. Glue on the 12, 3, 6, and 9 first, to get them in exactly the right position, then add medallions representing the remaining numbers. If desired, add press-on numerals to the clock.

~

Cost: $$$ Time: 2–3 hours Difficulty: moderate–hard

Ballet Class Picture

Any little girl who takes ballet will love these dainty ballerina figures made from flowers. Similar to the flower fairies (see pages 122–124), the ballerinas were created from bits and pieces of flowers. Their graceful arms and legs are made from the long, narrow stamens of cleome, or spider flower, and their hair is a combination of yellow marigold petals and Christmas fern roots. Once you have the basic images, scan them into the computer or have copies made so that you can use them to make iron-on transfers for decorating items such as pillows and bedsheets.

¼ yard of mordanted cloth
Stamens from cleome flower
Pink begonia petals
Christmas fern roots
Marigold petals
Petals from vinca, balloon flower, rose of Sharon, and zinnia
Mat with four openings, approximately 3 x 4 ½ inches each
Frame to fit mat (I used a 20 x 10 inch frame.)
Tape
Hammer
Iron

1. Practice with fabric scraps to determine how each petal transfers before you begin to "dress" your ballerinas.

2. For each figure, hammer a single pink begonia petal for the face and add a torso from a cleome petal (or small rose of Sharon petal). Next add the skirts. For these, I used: 10 zinnia petals, a single petal from rose of Sharon, 3 connected petals from the balloon flower, and 3 vinca petals. Trim or cut as needed, then hammer onto the fabric.

3. Use cleome stamens (the long, narrow, pink parts) to add arms and legs, positioning them as desired into ballet poses, and hammering them onto the fabric.

4. Add sleeves, if desired, cutting the petals to make them fit.

5. Make hair from curly roots or marigold petals and hammer them onto the fabric.

The ballet class

zinnia

rose of
Sharon

balloon
flower

vinca

6. Heat-set the images with the iron. Make copies or scan the figures into the computer to use for other projects.

7. Cut the figures out of the fabric, leaving several inches of fabric around each one, then tape the fabric to the mat, centering each figure in an opening.

8. Write on the mat, if desired, giving your figures a title and identifying each figure by the dominant flower. Then place the mat in the frame.

~

COST: $$$ (will vary with the frame used) TIME: 1–2 hours
DIFFICULTY: Easy to make the ballerinas, a little more skill to frame and add lettering to the mat

VARIATIONS ON A THEME

I took one of the scanned ballerina images, made an iron-on transfer, and ironed it onto a piece of cross-stitch fabric. I then filled in the design with appropriately colored embroidery cross-stitch to make a cute companion piece to the ballet class picture.

Herb Tiles

Although many of the common culinary herbs, such as mint, basil, oregano, and rosemary, do not make good candidates for hammered art, it is possible to bake these into polymer clay to make decorative tiles. I glued a series of three tiles to a jute ribbon, placed small bundles of the dried herbs in between, and hung it in the kitchen for a charming culinary decoration. You can use this same technique to make smaller tiles that are perfect as gift-box toppers for an herb lover.

Two 2-ounce packages of polymer clay
4–5 nice sage leaves
2–3 stems of parsley leaves
2–3 stems of thyme leaves and roots
Small bundles of herbs (I used sage, parsley, and thyme.)
Plastic wrap
Rolling pin
Wooden skewer, for writing in the clay (optional)
Foil-lined baking sheet
Olive-green acrylic paint (optional)
1 yard of 2-inch-wide jute ribbon for bow and for hanging
Several strands of raffia
Craft glue
Needle and thread (optional)
Picture hook
Oven
Hammer
Scissors

1. Place a small ball of clay on a piece of plastic wrap and roll out to ¼ inch thick.

2. Cut a 3-inch square out of the clay. Repeat until you have three squares.

3. Press or gently hammer one type of herb into each clay square. If desired, use the wooden skewer to write the name of the herb in the clay before you bake it.

4. Place the tiles on a foil-lined baking sheet and bake at 275°F for 10–15 minutes until hard. Do not let them begin to brown.

5. Remove the tiles from the oven and let cool. Note: when parsley and thyme baked, they remained in the clay. But the sage leaves shrank and pulled away from the clay, yet the texture of the leaf was beautifully detailed on the clay. So when the tile was cool, I removed all parts of the sage leaves and then made a thin wash from green acrylic paint and water and painted the indentations. I loved the effect!

6. Tie each herb bundle with raffia and make a decorative bow.

7. Cut a piece of jute ribbon about 17 inches long. Leave room at the top for a bow, then glue the tiles along the length of the ribbon, alternating the tiles and herb bundles.

8. Make a nice, flat bow for the top, and sew or glue a hook on the back for hanging.

~

Cost: $ Time: about 1 hour Difficulty: moderate

Flower Prints

Using the actual plant as a basis for fine art opens up a lot of design possibilities. There are drawbacks—the images must be used life sized and they can only be shown flat. You can vary the angle, but it's difficult to portray any kind of curling and twisting material.

Designing a piece to be hammered is easier than drawing from scratch because you can place the plants on your canvas or paper and get a good idea of what they will look like before you begin.

The technique is simple. I hammered the ferns (shown opposite) onto watercolor paper and hammered the bee balm (and some ferns), shown on page 81, onto mordanted linen. I then enhanced all of the images with acrylic paints. The directions following are for the fern print.

Hay Scented Fern
Dennstaedtia punctilobula

Adiantum pedatum
Northern Maidenhair Fern

16 x 20-inch piece of good-quality watercolor paper

1 or more fern pieces that fit gracefully onto the paper

Graphite pencil

Acrylic paints in fern colors

Artists's paintbrush

UV protective spray

Hammer

1. Place the fern pieces on the watercolor paper. Leave space at the bottom to draw in botanical details, such as roots or individual fronds. Leave space for both the common and botanical name, if desired.

2. Hammer the fern fronds. If you are layering fern pieces on top of one another, hammer the bottom fronds first. To obtain more of a 3-D look, place the first hammered fern images in the sunshine for a few hours before you hammer the second layer. This will make the bottom images a bit faded and help give more depth to the finished piece.

3. Mix acrylic paints to match the actual fern color and paint over the hammered images, using them as a guide. Use lighter paint shades on the bottom ferns and darker shades on the top ferns for the 3-D effect.

4. If desired, draw in more fern pieces. Then draw in magnified plant parts and/or add the names of the plants at the bottom of the print.

5. Spray the finished print with the UV spray before framing.

~

Cost: $ Time: 6–8 hours Difficulty: hard

VARIATIONS ON A THEME

You can create an equally charming botanical print by painting over images that have been hammered onto linen. While it is a bit more difficult to paint on linen than on watercolor paper, a greater variety of plant material transfers well to this fabric.

The bee balm print shown at right included a combination of ferns and bee balm flowers and leaves. I used tape to mask areas that I didn't want to paint—after I hammered the first layer of leaves, I covered them precisely with tape, cutting the tape to exactly match the leaf shapes. Then I hammered the next layer of leaves. The pigment won't go through the tape, and the result is a stunning 3-D look.

THE ART AND CRAFT OF POUNDING FLOWERS

Wearable Art

I knew I had reached the height of my hammering career when my mother called me to ask a favor: Would I hammer kudzu blossoms on the front of the evening dress she was wearing to celebrate her 60th wedding anniversary? It turned out beautifully (thank goodness!) and the dress was quite a conversation piece.

The images you can get from hammering plants to fabric are wonderful for decorating all kinds of clothing and accessories, from ball gowns to t-shirts. Whether you take the time to hammer images all over a length of fabric to make a dress, or you just hammer a single leaf or flower onto the collar of a blouse, your hammered art will make your clothing uniquely and beautifully yours. Many small accessories can be easily and quickly decorated with hammered images, for you to use yourself, give to friends, or sell to a local boutique. Here are some projects for you to try:

WOOL SCARF

SILK SCARF

RAW SILK SHAWL

CARROT-TOP TIE

FLORAL T-SHIRT

MAPLE LEAF T-SHIRT

GARDEN HAT

VIOLA BLOUSE

DECORATIVE BUTTONS

Botanical Scarves

Decorating scarves is an easy and effective way to use the art of hammered floral impressions. You can make a scarf out of a wide variety of fabrics—just let your creativity flow—you'll be amazed at the results!

Wool Scarf

A beautiful, lightweight scarf can be created from a length of wool, impressed with flowers of the season, and finished with fringed edges. Most wool comes in 56- to 60-inch widths, making it possible to create a scarf out of ⅓ yard (or even ¼ yard if you don't mind skinny scarves). Be mindful that this is not a rainy day scarf and should be protected from inclement weather.

Mordanted wool or mordanted heavy cotton (I used wool crepe.)
12-16 aster blossoms
Small bundle of carrot top leaves
Sewing machine or needle and thread
Hammer
Iron

1. Cut a piece of mordanted wool 9½ inches wide and 56–60 inches long. Be sure that you cut carefully and that the width remains exactly the same down the length of the scarf. Iron out all the wrinkles.

2. Position the carrot leaves on one end of the scarf, making a pleasing design. Hammer these onto the fabric a few at a time.

3. Place the aster blossoms at various places to give accent marks and bright spots of color. Hammer them onto the fabric.

4. Heat-set the images with the iron. Be sure not to heat too long, because green pigments on wool turn brown rapidly.

5. Using the sewing machine or needle and thread, stitch around all sides of the scarf, ½ inch in from the edge.

6. Carefully pull the edge threads to make fringe, beginning at the edge of the fabric and continuing to the stitching line.

~

COST: $$ TIME: 1–1½ hours   DIFFICULTY: moderate

Holiday Suggestion: For a Christmas scarf, hammer asparagus fern onto fabric and use small red satin bows as accents.

Silk Scarf

I found a wonderful sheer silk fabric composed of squares of slightly different shades. Although from a distance the fabric looks as if it is all cream colored, when you hold it up to the light, it becomes apparent that some of the squares are tinted with brown or green tones. I used a variety of spring blossoms to decorate the solid squares of this intriguing fabric and made scarves for friends and for myself.

⅓ yard of mordanted silk fabric, at least 54 inches wide and with a subtle pattern of squares
2 dozen or more small blossoms (I used viola, lobelia, and phlox.)
Sewing machine or needle and thread
Paper towels
Hammer
Iron

1. Trim the fabric so that it is exactly the same width down the length of the scarf and sew a narrow hem along the sides of the scarf.

2. Position the flowers on individual squares. You can decorate every square or concentrate the blossoms on each end.

3. When you are pleased with the arrangement, hammer the flowers onto the fabric one at a time, making sure to use paper towels underneath and on top of the silk.

4. Heat-set the images with the iron or have the scarf dry cleaned to set the pigments.

~

Cost: $ Time: 1–1½ hours Difficulty: moderate

Make It Simple: Purchase a ready-made plain white silk scarf to decorate with individual blossoms, or make iron-on transfers from a sheet of hammered images and iron the blossoms onto the silk. For information on making transfers, see pages 29–31.

Raw Silk Shawl

Cool summer evenings seem to be tailor-made for the elegance of a long, flowing shawl. Shawls are more graceful and easier to wear than sweaters or jackets, particularly over evening dresses or formal wear. Floral images, hammered onto silk or light cotton (or wool crepe, for a winter garment) make a stunning and beautiful wrap to complement your best dress. You can decorate the shawl wherever it pleases you, but the wide expanse of the back is a good place to show off large leaves or flowers.

Shawls are very easy to make, but if sewing is not your cup of tea, you can easily purchase a ready-made shawl to decorate with your favorite hammered images.

2 yards of good-quality silk, cotton, or lightweight wool, mordanted
  (Let the fabric run through your fingers before you purchase it to make certain
   that it drapes and folds gracefully; if you are buying expensive fabric, purchase
   just a sample to test for hammering.)
2 yards of lining fabric, matched as closely as possible to the fabric color
Large leaves and/or flowers for hammering (I used caladium leaves.)
2 yards of fringe or other trim (I used a 6-inch wide fringe, off-white to match the
   fabric; you could choose fringe or trim to match the colors of the image.)
Needle and thread or sewing machine
Pencil and paper
Hammer
Iron

Note: If you cannot wash the fabric, you cannot mordant it. Practice on a scrap of untreated fabric to determine if you can use it for hammered art. If the images fade quickly or change colors, or if the fabric will not take the hammering, one alternative is to use iron-on transfers (see pages 29–31). Another option is to make fabric appliqués out of the images and attach them to the shawl (see "Variations on a Theme" on page 90).

1. Iron the mordanted fabric to remove all wrinkles. Then cut the fabric into a rectangle measuring 64 inches long and 32 inches wide.

2. Cut the lining fabric to the same size and shape as the shawl fabric.

3. Practice hammering on a scrap of the shawl fabric to be sure the hammered images work. If your test is successful, place the leaves and/or flowers on the shawl, creating a pleasing design. You can decorate the back, the ends, or both. Make notes about where each plant goes or sketch your design on a piece of paper.

4. Remove the plants and then replace them on the fabric, one at a time. Hammer each plant until its image is completely transferred. Heat-set the images with the iron.

5. Place the lining over the shawl, right sides together, matching the outside edges.

6. Stitch on all four sides, leaving a 6-inch opening along one of the short ends.

7. Clip the corners and turn the shawl right side out, pulling through the opening. Press the edges with the iron.

8. Place the fringe or trim along the short end that has the opening. Stitch, being careful to sew the opening closed as you sew the fringe in place. Then sew the fringe in place at the opposite end of the shawl.

~

COST: $$$ TIME: 3–4 hours DIFFICULTY: moderate

VARIATIONS ON A THEME

If you don't want to hammer the images directly onto the fabric (or if your fabric will not take the images well) consider an alternative. Hammer the flowers or leaves onto a different fabric, scanning the design into the computer and printing it on fabric that you run through your printer (see "Duplicating the Images" on page 29). Cut out the images and appliqué them on the shawl. Note: Fabric that has been printed in a home printer is not waterfast, unless specially treated. Do not wash with water.

You can follow the shawl instructions to make a V-shaped shawl, which shows off the images beautifully. It is just as easy to make, but  you must cut the fabric into a triangle. Be sure that the tip of the triangle is in the center of the shawl. This can be a bit more expensive if you put fringe or trim along the long sides, because you'll need more fringe.

Carrot-Top Tie

I made this tie for my father, who loves to wear it to parties because he always ends up the center of attention! This is a fast and easy project, because ready-made white silk ties are available at most craft stores. Simply mordant the fabric, hammer the plants, and you've got an instant gift of wearable art.

Alum mordant
White silk tie
Carrot-top leaves and vinca blossoms (or leaves, ferns, or blossoms
    of your choice)
Pencil
Paper
Hammer
Iron

1. Mordant the tie and air dry thoroughly, being careful not to wrinkle the fabric.

2. Tie the tie as if you were wearing it so you can determine where the knot will be.

3. Place the tie on a hammering surface, with the front of the tie facing you. Position the carrot leaves and vinca blossoms on the front of the tie until you have a design you like. Make sure that the heavier part of your design (either the darkest colors or the busiest part of the design) is at the bottom of the tie, getting lighter and more delicate toward the top.

4. Make notes about your design or make a rough sketch of it, then remove the plant material.

5. Practice on the narrow (back) end of the tie, hammering a tiny piece of the plant material to make sure that your plants transfer well.

6. When you're satisfied with your design and hammering techniques, hammer each piece of plant onto the tie separately, taping as necessary to get a better design on the silk.

7. Heat-set the images with the iron. Be careful not to burn the design or the silk.

~

Cost: $$ Time: less than an hour Difficulty: easy to moderate

Floral T-Shirt

Brightly colored spring flowers seem ready-made for decorating a t-shirt. Since I wanted to be able to wash the shirt and have the flower images last a long time, I used iron-on transfers instead of hammering directly onto the fabric.

Good-quality white t-shirt
At least 9 different floral or leaf images, printed on iron-on transfer paper (I used lobelia, thrift, dianthus, pink oxalis, viola, blue phlox, a red maple leaf, fern, ajuga, and a mini rose.)
Tracing paper
Fabric transfer paper (available at craft and fabric stores)
Ruler
Fabric marker or paint
Pins
Hammer
Iron

1. Wash the t-shirt, using a mild detergent. Dry, but do not use dryer sheets. It is not necessary to use a mordant on the fabric, since you are using impressions from iron-on transfers.

2. Iron the t-shirt to remove all wrinkles.

3. On a piece of tracing paper, draw a 7½-inch square. Divide this into three rows of three squares each. Each square should measure 2½ inches. Be sure that each individual image will fit into this size square. If your flowers are larger, adjust the size of the squares. (See photo opposite.)

4. Lay the t-shirt out on a flat surface. Place the nine-square design on the t-shirt, making sure that it is centered. Pin it into place.

5. Take fabric transfer paper and slip it between the design and the t-shirt. Using a pencil or specially made marker, transfer the design to the t-shirt by tracing over the design.

6. Using a fabric marker, draw in the lines for your nine-square design. Use a straightedge ruler and do this carefully. It's a good idea to practice on t-shirt fabric before you do it on the real shirt.

7. Cut out the iron-on transfer images as precisely as possible, leaving little of the background paper.

8. Place one image in each of the nine squares, moving them about until you are satisfied with the design. Leave room for the plant name, if desired. Remember that you place the transfers face down on the fabric, meaning the transfers will actually be a mirror image when you iron them on.

9. Remove the images from the t-shirt, keeping them in the correct order. One at a time, place each image in its designated square and iron the image onto the fabric.

10. Use the fabric marker to write the name of each flower, if desired.

11. When it's time to wash the t-shirt, either wash by hand, dry clean, or turn the shirt inside out and wash in cold water on the delicate cycle. Machine-dry on the gentle cycle.

~

COST: $$$ TIME: 2-3 hours DIFFICULTY: moderate

Maple Leaf T-Shirt

The brilliant colors of autumn leaves can be captured on a stunning t-shirt made from a tree silhouette and Japanese maple leaves. The images are iron-on transfers created from hammering bright leaves onto cloth and copying them onto appropriate fabric. Using iron-on transfers allows the shirt to be washed in the washing machine and makes it relatively lightfast.

Good-quality cotton t-shirt
Tree silhouette pattern (see page 96)
Tracing paper
Fabric transfer paper
Fabric paint or pens, brown and black
Iron-on transfers, created from 10–12 hammered images of small maple leaves
    (no larger than 3 x 3 inches)
Paper or cardboard
Ruler
Hammer
Iron

1. Use a piece of tracing paper to trace the tree silhouette below. Enlarge it on a copier 100–200 percent, depending on the size of your shirt. Take the traced image and put it exactly in the center of the back of the t-shirt. Use a ruler to measure so the pattern is centered on the t-shirt. Then use the fabric transfer paper to trace over the silhouette and get the design on the shirt.

2. Once the tree pattern is on the shirt, place a piece of paper or cardboard inside the shirt to keep the colors from bleeding through, and color in the silhouette with the brown or black fabric paint or pen.

3. Cut out the iron-on transfer images as precisely as possible, leaving little of the background paper.

4. Put a board or hard surface inside the shirt. Then place an iron-on leaf image, color side down, at an appropriate spot on the silhouette, and iron it onto the fabric. Continue ironing leaf images over the tree silhouette until you are pleased with the overall design. Use a single leaf image on the front of the shirt, on the pocket, or upper right side, if desired.

~

Cost: $$$ Time: 1–3 hours Difficulty: moderate

Make It Simple: Purchase a t-shirt and decorate it by using iron-on transfer images on the pocket, on the collar, or around the neckline.

Garden Hat

*J*ust iron the images of your choice onto the bill of the cap and there you go! This is a quick and unique hat to wear for all your gardening chores, from weeding to showing off your perennial borders. Although I chose to use the images only on the bill of the cap, you could also iron some onto the front.

White cotton cap (available at craft stores)
Iron-on transfers, created from hammered images of flowers
Iron

1. Position the images on the hat. You can center them, decorate one side or another, or cover the bill with the flowers of your choice.

2. When you are pleased with your design, remove the images and iron them onto the cap one at a time.

~

Cost: $ Time: 15 minutes Difficulty: easy

Viola Blouse

*T*his delicate silk blouse looks absolutely beautiful with the small violas printed around the neckline. Remember that you must dry clean this garment, because the images will not hold well if they get wet.

Silk shell or blouse (If you are sewing a blouse, purchase ¼–½ yard extra for practicing or for recutting, in case you don't get a good impression the first time.)

Small flowers that make very good impressions, such as violas, small pansies, lobelia, or verbena (or leaves such as blackberry, kudzu, asparagus fern, other ferns)

Alum, for mordanting

Straight pins

Pen

Paper towels

Hammer

Iron

1. Mordant the garment or the fabric (see "Pretreating Fabrics" on pages 23–24). Dry thoroughly. If your garment says "Dry Clean Only," test to see how your flowers transfer without mordanting.

2. Practice making hammered impressions on the fabric you will be using. If you're using a ready-made blouse, practice on a shirt tail, a facing—anywhere that won't show. You might even want to take a few stitches out of a hem and fold it down to hammer on.

3. Decide where you want to place your impressions. If you are making your own blouse, place the front pattern piece on a table and

position the flowers until you are pleased with the design. Mark their placement on the pattern piece. Remove the plants and pin the pattern piece to the fabric. Mark the neck and shoulder lines with dressmaker's transfer or a pen with washable ink. Remove the pattern piece.

If you are using a store-bought garment, position the flowers or leaves until you are pleased with the design, then make notes about the design or make a quick sketch and remove the plants.

4. Place the garment or marked fabric (don't cut out the pattern piece yet) on a hammering surface. Be sure to place paper towels both underneath and on top of the fabric. Double

check to see that the flower or leaf is exactly where you need it to be, then hammer. Repeat with the other plant parts until the design is finished. One advantage to making your blouse is that if, for any reason, your impressions do not turn out well, you can begin again. Simply re-mark the fabric and hammer the flowers in the appropriate space. Then cut out the pattern piece and continue to sew the blouse according to the pattern directions.

If your impression doesn't come out well on a ready-made blouse, you'll have to cover it with an appliquéd image made on another piece of fabric (see "Variations on a Theme" on page 90).

5. Heat-set the images with the iron or have the garment dry cleaned immediately.

~

COST: $$$ TIME: 20 minutes (if you use a store-bought blouse, considerably longer if you sew it yourself)
DIFFICULTY: easy (unless you sew it yourself)

Decorative Buttons

Using hammered cloth to cover buttons is an easy way to make stunning accent pieces for clothing. Plain metal button forms are readily found at fabric or craft stores and come with clear instructions and a pattern for cutting the cloth just the right size.

Metal button forms
Small hammered impressions on fabric, such as small violas or lobelia

1. Follow the button package instructions for cutting the fabric and placing it on the button form.

2. Use the buttons as accents on clothing or accessories, particularly those made with other hammered images. The buttons can be used on pillows, cushions, and slipcovers—use your imagination to come up with some interesting ideas for these unique and beautiful notions.

~

COST: $ TIME: 10 minutes per button DIFFICULTY: easy

VARIATIONS ON A THEME

An alternative to making cloth-covered buttons is to make buttons from polymer clay; the advantage is that you can make them any size or shape you need. Clay buttons are so quick and easy to make that you can "cook up" dozens in no time. Simply mold a small amount of clay until it is about ¼-inch thick, shape it, press in the flower of your choice, add a buttonhook on the back, and bake. (For more information about using polymer clay, see pages 38–39.)

Gifts and Accessories

*H*ammered art offers endless possibilities for making gifts for friends, family, and yourself. Many of the craft projects in this chapter can be finished in 15 minutes or less, and some are so easy that children can create them with just a bit of help. The most difficult part about crafting these gifts will be giving them away. Here are some great gift ideas:

POTPOURRI BAGS

BABY BIB AND SOCKS

SILK EYEGLASS CASE

GARDEN JOURNAL

VACATION SCRAPBOOK

BEE BALM CROSS-STITCH

CLAY MAGNETS

PICTURE FRAME

FLOWER FAIRY BOOK

BINDER COVER

JEWELRY PINS

Potpourri Bags

Potpourri—the wonderful combination of sweetly scented petals, spices, and herbs—can be beautifully wrapped in small squares of fabric and adorned with hammered images. Make the potpourri yourself out of your garden's bounty, or buy it ready-made.

I filled one of the bags with dried dill leaves and decorated it by hammering on a sprig of dill—a symbol of good cheer. I filled another bag with potpourri and decorated it with aster, which, according to legend, is a talisman of love made from starlight.

¼ yard of plain white or off-white fabric (will make at least 10 bags)

Sprigs of dill and aster blossoms, or other leaves and flowers, for hammering

Alum for mordanting (optional)

2 tablespoons of dried leaves, petals, or potpourri

½ yard of ½-inch satin ribbon (red for dill, purple for aster)

Pinking shears (optional)

Sewing machine or needle and thread

Hammer

Iron

Scissors

1. Practice hammering your chosen plants on a fabric scrap to see if you like the effect on untreated fabric. If you do, then don't mordant the fabric. Otherwise, mordant the fabric with an alum bath (see "Pretreating Fabrics" on pages 23–24 for details).

2. Cut two 3 x 5-inch pieces out of the fabric and iron them.

3. Position the dill sprigs and aster blossoms (or leaves and flowers of your choice) on the fabric pieces and hammer them.

4. Heat-set the images with the iron.

5. Place the fabric pieces with decorated sides together and stitch down the sides and across the bottom, using a ½-inch seam. Turn under the raw edges at the top or cut the top edges with pinking shears. Turn the bag right side out.

HERB AND FLOWER SYMBOLISM

Chrysanthemum: cheerfulness

Clover (4-leaf): good luck

Coreopsis: love at first sight

Fern: fascination

Forget-me-not: friendship

Lily of the valley: return of happiness

Honeysuckle: bond of love

Parsley: festivity

Queen Anne's lace: self-reliance

Rose: love

Rosemary: remembrance

Rue: protection from evil

Thyme: courage

Violet (and viola): faithfulness

6. Put the potpourri into the bag and tie it shut with the ribbon. Make a bow with long, graceful tails. If you wish, you can make a small card to go with the bag, explaining the symbolism of the plants you've used (see "Herb and Flower Symbolism" above).

~

COST: $ TIME: about 10 minutes per bag DIFFICULTY: easy

Baby Bib and Socks

These adorable accessories were so quick and easy to make, I could have turned out many more in just one day! I bought the bib from a craft store for $1.29 and got the little socks at the grocery store for about twice that amount. I had a few iron-on transfer images left over from another project. So for less than $4.00 and in about 15 minutes, I put together a great gift for a friend's newborn baby.

5 to 6 iron-on transfer images (I used phlox and violas; for something more frilly, you could use pink oxalis, rose petals, or dianthus.)
Baby bib
Baby socks
Iron
Scissors

1. Cut out the iron-on transfer images as precisely as possible, leaving little of the background paper.

2. Place the bib flat on an ironing board or other firm surface. Position the flower transfers in a pleasing design.

3. Iron the transfer images onto the bib, one at a time.

4. Decorate the socks, ironing on one flower image on the outside of each cuff.

~

COST: $$ TIME: 10–15 minutes   DIFFICULTY: easy

Holiday Suggestion: Make festive holiday baby accessories by using asparagus fern transfers—they look just like miniature Christmas trees!

Silk Eyeglass Case

Make a personal statement with a one-of-a-kind eyeglass case. You can find plain silk cases in a craft store, in the silk-painting section. Simply hammer on the plant or flower image of your choice, and you've got an instant gift.

Silk eyeglass case
Mini rose blossoms and leaves, or plant material of your choice
Aluminum foil
Scotch tape
Wooden cutting board
Hammer

1. Put the case on a wooden cutting board. Position the blossoms and leaves, moving them about until you are satisfied with the look. Tape the petals on top of the case in the desired spot.

2. Place a piece of aluminum foil inside the case to prevent the transfer from going all the way through to the back.

3. Hammer the petals thoroughly. (Because the eyeglass case is already padded, there is no need to put paper towels under the plants.) Taping the petals on top helps keep them in place. It's difficult to get a crisp, clean transfer on a silk case, but you will get a soft, "impressionistic" transfer that is quite attractive.

~

Cost: $ Time: about 20 minutes Difficulty: easy

BEAUTIFUL BAGS

You can create all kinds of beautiful bags using the same technique described at left. Cosmetic bags, pencil bags, tote bags, lunch bags, and even backpacks can all be decorated with hammered flowers, ferns, or leaves. Follow the directions for the eyeglass case, but instead of taping the plant materials in place, simply position them on the outside of the bag, cover with a paper towel or piece of plastic wrap, and hammer.

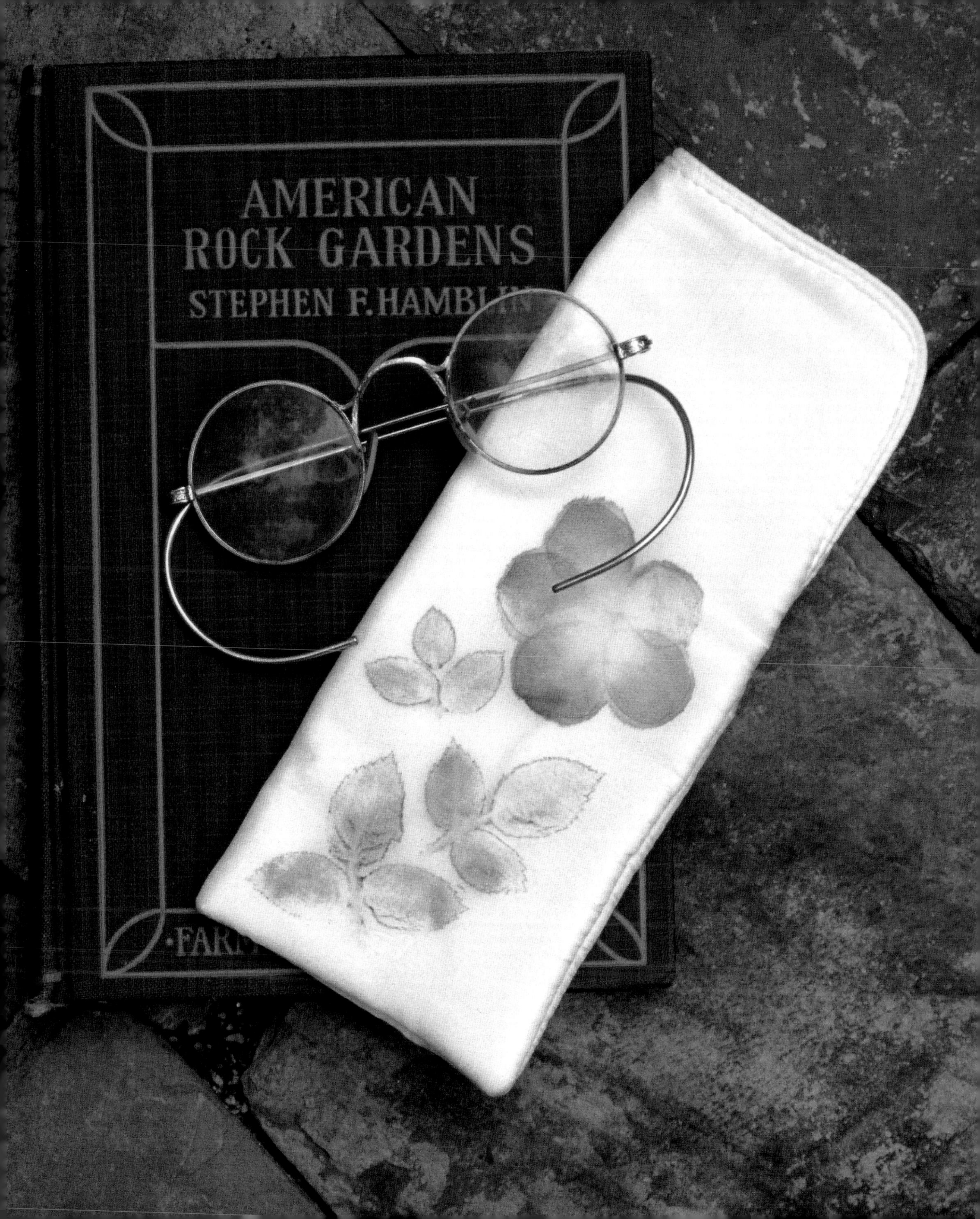
AMERICAN
ROCK GARDENS
STEPHEN F.

Garden Journal

This journal is a wonderful project to make with children or with a class of adults who are interested in journaling. The variations are endless—write haiku or poetry and illustrate it with hammered flowers; make a garden diary of plants that you have included in your own garden; or create a nature journal, decorating the pages with hammered plants that you found on your walks through the woods.

Blank book of watercolor paper, with either back or front cover of heavy cardboard
  (Be sure to buy watercolor paper—it will take impressions from many more types of flowers
  than regular paper.)
Heavy colored papers
Narrow double-sided tape
Small pieces of cloth
Watercolor paper, mulberry paper (available at craft stores), or other absorbent paper
Twigs, vines, woodland treasures for collage (optional)
Craft glue or glue stick
Fusible webbing (optional)
Hammer
Scissors or craft knife

1. Choose a blank book that has at least one heavy cardboard cover. It doesn't matter if it's the front or back cover, but turn the book so that the heaviest cover is the front.

2. Measure the cover and cut a piece of heavy colored paper the exact height and twice the width of the cover, excluding the binding. For example, my book is 5 inches high, and (from the inside edge of the spiral binding) 7¾ inches wide. So I cut a piece of colored paper exactly 5 x 15½ inches for the front cover. Fold the paper in half and crease.

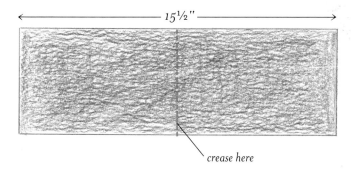

15½"

crease here

3. Take narrow double-sided tape and carefully put it down the edge of the spiral binding and the other three edges of the outside cover.

4. Take the creased colored paper and open it up, with the crease facing away from you, so the paper will stand up like a tent. Line up the left-hand edge of the paper with the left-hand edge of the front book cover and attach the paper to the cover.

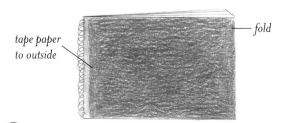

tape paper to outside

fold

5. Open the journal and repeat the process of applying tape to the inside of the cover. Then fold the remaining colored paper over and apply pressure to adhere the paper to the inside cover.

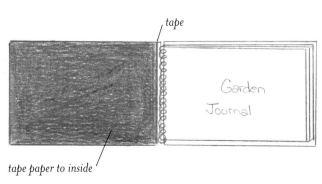

tape

Garden Journal

tape paper to inside

6. Your cover is now ready for decorating. You can do this any way that pleases you. I chose to make a collage of graduated sizes of papers and fabric, framed with woodland treasures. To do the same, cut a piece of colored paper (I used green) just slightly smaller than the size of the front cover. If you want torn edges, wet the paper where you want it torn, then tear carefully.

7. Use a glue stick and glue the paper to the cover.

8. Cut a piece of decorated watercolor or mulberry paper (see "Decorated Papers" at right) slightly smaller than the colored paper and glue it to the cover.

9. Create a single, perfect image on a piece of white fabric. This will be the centerpiece of your cover. My central image is 3½ x 4 inches. I hammered a passionflower leaf. You might have to make several images before you get one you're thrilled with, but keep working because it's worth the effort to create a beautiful cover. When you're happy with the image, use either glue or fusible webbing to adhere it to the center of the cover, on top of the decorated paper.

10. If you like, frame the fabric image using pieces of ribbon, twine, raffia, or small sticks. I used thin pieces of the greenbrier vine because I loved the tendrils I found on it.

~

COST: $–$$$ TIME: ongoing project (could take days or months) DIFFICULTY: easy–hard

Make It Simple: Hammer an image onto a piece of fabric or heavy paper and glue it to the front of the book. Embellish with bits of glued-on sticks, moss, or shells.

DECORATED PAPERS

Mulberry paper, available at many art-supply and craft stores, is a wonderful material for hammering. Although thin, it is absorbent, and takes images well, making it perfect to use in a variety of crafts. Not only did I use this paper for the front cover of my journal, but I also used it as endpapers for the inside front and back covers.

The most important—and most difficult—part about creating an overall cover design is to make it random. You don't want rows or patterns (unless you plan to measure and make your rows and patterns perfectly even). You can use anything that appeals to you and that you have available. Just check to make sure that the image takes well to the paper before you begin. For the cover paper, I used a combination of dill leaves and individual verbena petals. For the inside end pages I used Queen Anne's lace leaves and dahlia petals.

Vacation Scrapbook

*H*ammered images make perfect illustrations for a scrapbook. I made a book about my trip to the Smoky Mountains last fall. I hammered leaves and field flowers onto the pages, or sometimes onto fabric, to remind me of the beautiful scenes that we saw along the way. You can use just hammered images or combine them with photographs and memorabilia to create a book of memories.

Assorted plant materials
Scrapbook, at least 8½ x 11 inches, with heavy paper
Cloth and special paper for hammering images
Glue stick, craft glue, or fusible webbing
Memorabilia from your trip—maps, brochures, bumper stickers, receipts, etc.
Large envelope for keeping memorabilia together
Photographs
Pieces of watercolor paper or mordanted fabric for hammering
Hammer
Iron

1. Gather plants wherever possible and keep them in a plastic bag in a cooler until you make a stop and can hammer them.

2. Hammer the plants onto the pages. Then add your trip memorablia, write notes, etc. (see "Putting It All Together" at right). Use your field guide to identify the plants that you see and, as you hammer them, make notes about their names and where they were growing. Your scrapbook could actually become your field guide, not only reminding you of a fun trip, but also as a guide to the plants growing in a particular locale at a certain season. You might want to follow the same route during a different season and see how the plants have changed.

3. You'll quickly find out that not all plants transfer well and some will do better on fabric than they do on paper, so you'll need to be flexible in putting your pages together. The last couple of pages of my trip book are testing pages, where I take a leaf or petal and try it out on a scrap of paper before I hammer it onto a clean, new sheet. I also have scraps of fabric that I keep in a plastic insert sheet at the back of the book for the same purpose. I first try the plants on paper and if they don't work, then I try them on cotton. As you experiment, remember to vary the padding both underneath and on top to get as clear an image as possible.

~

Cost: $$$ Time: ongoing project Difficulty: easy

Kudzu   Pueraria lobata

Location: Parking lot Red Top Mountain
Date: September 8

Kudzu is everywhere - covers trees, bu
passed miles and miles of the stuff
It seems to crawl over anything in
It was brought to the South to control
out of hand. Even though it's terric
a beautiful flower. Even though
pinkish-purple, it turned a beau
I hammered it on wool that ha

Actual Color

PUTTING IT ALL TOGETHER

Hammering directly onto the scrapbook paper is, of course, the easiest way to illustrate your book, but not all plants yield successful images. Your alternative is to hammer onto watercolor paper or fabric instead. Just be sure that your image is not larger than your scrapbook page. Here are a couple of ways to put your scrapbook together:

- If you can add pages to your scrapbook, use plastic insert pages that are open at the top. Hammer your images onto fabric, heat-set them with the iron, and slip the illustrated fabric into the plastic sleeve. Use a small piece of tape at the top to adhere the fabric to the inside of the sleeve so it doesn't slip or fold over. Or hammer the image onto watercolor paper and slip the paper into the sleeve.

- Hammer your images onto fabric or paper, then cut them out and adhere them directly to a page in the scrapbook. Use a glue stick that is made for both paper and fabric. Or use double-sided tape to mount the image. If you're working with fabric, another option is to use fusible webbing to adhere the image to the scrapbook page.

- Enhance the pages with pieces of memorabilia from the trip—maps and brochures are great, as are ticket stubs and postcards.

- Take photographs to go along with your hammered images. A picture of a field of flowers next to the hammered image of a single specimen makes a stunning combination.

Bee Balm Cross-Stitch

One of the interesting ways you can use hammered flower images is to create your own designs for needlepoint, embroidery, and cross-stitch. You can choose from a wider variety of flowers when making these crafts because it doesn't matter if the pigments fade—you're only using the images to create a pattern that you will embellish with thread or yarn. (See "Variations on a Theme" on page 75.)

Hammer the flowers directly onto a white canvas for needlepoint or cross-stitch, or onto white fabric for embroidery work. An alternative is to hammer your images onto smooth, tightly woven fabric and copy them onto iron-on transfer paper as described below. This allows you to manipulate the size of the images and use them again and again in any design.

> White 14-count cross-stitch canvas, 8 x 10 inches
> Embroidery floss—3 shades of green, 4 shades of pink
> Bee balm flowers, leaves, and sepals, (or flowers and leaves of your choice)
> 8½ x 11-inch white, tightly woven mordanted cotton or linen
> Scanner, computer, printer, iron-on transfer paper (optional)
> Hammer
> Iron

1. Hammer the bee balm flowers onto the large piece of mordanted cotton or linen. Be certain that the image is not larger than your scanner (or copier) will hold.

2. Scan the fabric into the computer, reducing or enlarging the image, if desired. Print on iron-on transfer paper. Or take your hammered image to a copy shop and have copies made onto iron-on transfer paper.

3. Cut out the iron-on transfer images as precisely as possible, leaving little of the background paper. Then iron the images onto the cross-stitch canvas.

4. Use the embroidery floss to stitch lighter-colored highlights, veins, and details first, followed by darker outlines. Use contrasting lights and darks to give depth to the design.

~

Cost: $ Time: about 1 hour to hammer image (many hours to execute design) Difficulty: easy–hard

Clay Magnets

$\mathcal{D}$ecorating plastic clay with plants is an easy, great rainy day activity for children. By gluing small magnets to the backs, you can create an assortment of decorative magnets.

1 small lump of polymer clay (about the size of a ping pong ball) for each magnet

Plastic wrap

Rolling pin

Small flowers, leaves, or ferns that fit within the cookie cutter

Small round or square cookie cutter

Polymer clay glaze

Small paintbrush

Small magnets

Craft glue or hot glue gun

Oven

Aluminum foil

Baking sheet

GET CREATIVE WITH CLAY

Polymer clay can be the basis for a variety of crafts, from magnets to buttons (see page 101) to Christmas tree ornaments (see page 144). Follow directions for magnets, altering the size and shape of your clay creations as desired. Because plant materials are simply pressed into the clay and baked, these crafts are perfect to do with children.

1. Place a large piece of plastic wrap on your work surface. Put one lump of clay on the plastic and roll it out until it is smooth and approximately $\frac{1}{4}$ inch thick.

2. Position the plants into the clay, making sure that they fit within the edges of the cookie cutter. Cover with another piece of plastic wrap and gently roll, hammer, or press the plants into the clay.

3. Place the cookie cutter over the plants and press down. Remove the clay "cookie" and smooth out the edges, if necessary. Set aside.

Continue making clay cookies until you have the number desired.

4. Cut a piece of foil to fit on the baking sheet. Place the clay cookies on the foil. (Do not bake directly on surfaces that will be used for baking food.) Bake in 275°F oven for about 10 minutes or until the pieces are hard but have not begun to turn brown. Do not overbake.

5. Allow the pieces to cool. Use a small paintbrush to apply at least one coat of glaze.

6. After the glaze has dried, glue a small magnet to the back of each piece.

~

COST: $ TIME: 20 minutes DIFFICULTY: easy

Picture Frame

Polymer clay "tiles" can be used to decorate a plain picture frame and make it look extraordinary. Remember that both the baking and the glazing process change the color of many plants (see the list on page 39). It's a good idea to experiment with the plants you have available before you make finished tiles.

About 1 pound of polymer clay

Rolling pin

Straightedge or ruler

Picture frame with wide frame pieces (My frame is 7 x 9 inches; the opening is 5½ x 3½ inches, and the frame pieces are 1¾ inches wide.)

Hot glue or craft glue

10 or more small plant pieces (each no more than 2-inch square; I used black-eyed Susan, tiny pine tree, orange zinnia, walking fern, Christmas fern, yellow coreopsis, Japanese maple leaf, coleus leaves, butter daisy, Queen Anne's lace.)

Plastic wrap

Oven

Aluminum foil

Baking sheet

Inexpensive paintbrush

Polymer clay glaze

Hammer

1. Cover your work surface with plastic wrap and roll out the clay to a thickness of about ¼ inch.

2. Using a straightedge or ruler, cut the clay into ten 2-inch squares. You might have to work in two different batches to do this, unless your work surface is very large.

3. Choose small plants and leaves to fit onto the tiles. Gently press or hammer the plants into the tile pieces. If the tile pieces get bigger as you push on them, be sure to trim them to exactly 2 inches square again.

VARIATIONS ON A THEME

Decorated picture frames are perfect for showing off hammered art. In addition to using clay tiles, you can also embellish store-bought frames with paper or fabric that has been decorated with hammered images. Simply hammer leaves, ferns, or flowers onto a piece of paper or fabric and cut it to fit around the face of the picture frame. Fold the edges of the paper or fabric toward the back of the frame and glue it in place. You can enhance the effect by using hammered art to decorate the mat, as well.

4. Cover the baking sheet with a piece of aluminum foil. Put the tiles on the foil and bake at 275°F for 10–12 minutes. Do not allow them to begin to brown. When the pieces are hard, remove them from the oven and allow to cool.

5. Use the paintbrush to brush on the polymer clay glaze. Add a second coat of glaze, if necessary.

6. Glue the tiles to the outside of the frame, spacing them evenly. If they hang off the side of the frame a little, that's not a problem. Insert a favorite photograph and display.

~

COST: $$ TIME: 1–2 hours DIFFICULTY: moderate

Flower Fairy Book

There are a number of charming books about "Flower Fairies" in which paintings or drawings of various petals and plants have been used to create figures that look like fairies. You can do the same thing, only you can use the actual flowers to make your fairies and other figures. You'll never look at flowers again in the same way. Suddenly the petals of rose of Sharon can be nothing but the skirt to a fancy gown, while the single curved petals of pink impatiens will forever after look like the puffed sleeves of a party dress.

Making the faces, arms, legs, shoes, and hair was a matter of trial and error. I found that a single petal of a pink begonia was perfect for a pink face. Slender stalks of nandina with a single pointed leaf still attached made good high-heeled slippers. And hair? The root of Christmas fern provided the best material. As for arms and legs, the stamens of cleome are perfect! But, as with every project, these are only starting points. Use your imagination to find plant material for the best little fairies in the garden. *Note:* This same idea was used to create the series of ballerinas shown on page 74.

Linen or cotton, mordanted (each figure takes two 4 x 6-inch fabric pieces)
Leaves and flowers
Photo album, approximately 5 x 6 inches, with plastic sleeves for protecting photographs
Colored paper for cover, approximately 12 x 14 inches
Double-sided tape or glue
Fusible webbing
Hammer
Iron
Scissors

1. Iron the mordanted fabric to get out all the wrinkles. Then cut the fabric into 4 x 6-inch pieces. You'll need two pieces for each figure.

2. Create the figure by laying plant pieces on the fabric. Start with the face, then add the dress. Test out various flowers and leaves by laying them on the figure, as if you're dressing a paper doll.

3. When you are satisfied with your figure, hammer all the individual parts into place.

4. Take the other piece of cut fabric and hammer the same plants individually (ones used for hair, face, shoes, skirt, etc.), and label each one with the name of the flower or plant.

5. Place the decorated fabric pieces in the photo album sleeves. Arrange so that you see the

figure on one side and the flowers used to create her on the other.

6. Cut a piece of colored paper two inches wider and two inches longer than the total dimensions of the album (including front and back).

7. Place the opened album on top of the paper and fold in on all sides, making a book cover with 1-inch flaps on the inside of the book.

8. Trim the corners, then fold in (as if you were wrapping a package). Put double-sided tape (or glue) around the inside edge of the album, then fold the paper to the inside, covering the entire cover, front and back.

9. Choose a favorite flower fairy for the cover. Use fusible webbing to adhere the fabric fairy to the paper and cover the raw edges with a trim of paper or fabric. Either write a title on the cover or print one and glue it to the front.

I put the following poem in the front of my book:

Make your own fairies
with flowers and leaves.
Use petals and ferns
to make blouses with sleeves.
With larkspur for hats
and zinnias for shoes,
you can make a wee kingdom
from the flowers you choose.

~

Cost: $–$$$ Time: varies (depending on how many pages there are and how elaborate you make your book) Difficulty: moderate

---

MAKING FLOWER FAIRIES

Fairies, gnomes, and other wee folk can be created from a variety of flowers and leaves. Once you begin creating these fantasy creatures, it's hard to stop! Here are some suggestions for plants to use for the various body parts of these fantasy creatures:

Hair: blonde hair from strips of marigold or coreopsis, brown hair from roots of fern
Wings: coleus leaves, balloon flower petals

Faces: begonia petals
Legs and arms: stamens from cleome, strips of coleus petals, bee balm petals
Shirts and blouses: Stokes aster, small maple leaf, fern, dill, dahlia petals, vinca petals
Skirts: ferns, rose of Sharon, coleus leaves, coreopsis petals
Shoes: nandina leaves, pieces of vinca blossoms, zinnia blossoms

Binder Cover

This is one of my easiest projects. You can make a dozen of these for gifts in no time at all. The key is to start with a good hammered image of a large leaf of flower, or combinations of leaves and flowers. Then you simply make color copies of this and use it for your cover. I used a fern for one and three caladium leaf images on another.

Large leaf, flower, or fern, or combination of several
White fabric, 8½ x 11 inches
Binder with clear sleeve on cover
Hammer
Color copier or printer

1. Hammer the plant material onto the fabric. If you want to decorate several binders, make color copies of the hammered image.

2. Slip either the original hammered fabric or the color copies into the clear sleeve on the binder front. That's it!

~

Cost: $$ Time: 5 minutes Difficulty: very easy

Jewelry Pins

Flowers are truly the jewels of nature, so why not take advantage of the exquisite beauty of blossoms and leaves and hammer their images to wear as pins on your favorite dress or jacket? These are quick and easy to make and are perfect "thank you" gifts or holiday stocking stuffers. Older children will like making these pins for teachers' gifts or to give to friends.

4-inch square of cotton fabric for each pin
Small leaf or flower for each pin
Fusible webbing
Fusible vinyl
4-inch square of very stiff interfacing for each pin
Metal pin backing (available at craft stores)
Hot glue or craft glue
Hammer
Iron
Scissors

1. Hammer the plant materials onto the fabric. If you aren't pleased with the results, use mordanted fabric.

2. Cut out the image, leaving a 1-inch margin of fabric all around.

3. Using the cut-out image as a pattern, cut out the same size and shape from the fusible webbing and the fusible vinyl.

4. Place the back side of the image to the sticky side of the webbing. Press with the iron for 2 to 3 seconds.

5. Remove the paper backing and place the image on the interfacing. Do not iron yet. Remove the paper from the back of the fusible vinyl and smooth the vinyl onto the image. Place the protective paper over the vinyl and iron for 8 seconds. Carefully turn the entire piece over and, again using the protective paper, iron for an additional 8 seconds on the back side. When you are through, you should have the image sandwiched between the fusible webbing and the vinyl.

6. Allow the piece to cool, then cut out the image, following its shape exactly so that there is no fabric around it. Glue the pin backing to the back of the pin.

~

Cost: $ Time: 15 minutes per pin Difficulty: easy

Celebration Ware

Flowers have long been a part of almost all celebrations, from holidays and birthdays to graduations and anniversaries. Since sending fresh flowers is not always practical, you can transfer the rich red of roses, gorgeous green of ferns, and brilliant blue of lobelia to paper or fabric, and make your own celebration ware. Hammered art is perfect for making greeting cards and wrapping paper, and for decorating table linens and ornaments suitable for any celebration. Brighten up festive occasions with the following projects:

GREETING CARDS

ROSE CARD

ACCORDIAN-FOLD BOOK

CALLING CARDS AND GIFT TAGS

CHRISTMAS WREATH CARD

CLOTH CHRISTMAS ORNAMENTS

CLAY CHRISTMAS ORNAMENTS

CHRISTMAS NAPKINS

CHRISTMAS STOCKING

GIFT BAGS

WRAPPING PAPER AND RIBBONS

Greeting Cards

If you love to send cards, make them yourself! You get the pleasure of creating them and your friends and family get the fun of receiving one-of-a-kind pieces of art.

The easiest and quickest cards are made by hammering flowers directly onto paper. Just remember to test your plant material before you start hammering on a blank card. Unfortunately, not all flowers transfer well and only a few leaves give good impressions on paper. Different papers take the transfers in different ways, so a little testing is definitely in order. For best results, use cards made from a thick, absorbent paper, such as watercolor paper.

CARD-MAKING OPTIONS

If you hammer an image you really love, you can use it over and over again by making color copies. Do this at home by scanning the image into the computer, then running it through a color printer. If you don't have this equipment, or if you want a better quality color print than you can get at home, take your image to a copy shop and get copies made.

Once you have a nice color copy, you can either trim it to fit your card or you can cut it smaller and put a "frame" of colored paper behind it. Use a glue stick to adhere the paper to the card. If you find it easier to hammer onto fabric than to paper, or if you want to use flowers that transfer better to fabric, it's easy to create a card using fabric. (This also allows you to use less-expensive plain note cards rather than watercolor cards.) Mordant, dry, and iron your fabric (see

pages 23–24 for details). Then hammer the images to make a pleasing design. Trim the decorated fabric the same size as the card front.

You can adhere the fabric to the card by using a glue stick or a liquid craft glue—just be sure that you cover the back of the fabric evenly with glue, using a small paintbrush, so you won't see "glue trails" when it dries. My favorite method is to use fusible webbing, which offers a beautiful, smooth finish. Cut a piece of webbing (available at craft and fabric stores) the same size as the fabric, then follow the manufacturer's directions and adhere the fabric to the front of the card. If the edges begin to come loose, you can glue them down. Glue a strip of narrow ribbon around the edge of the card, covering the raw edges of the fabric (see the Rose Card on pages 134–135 for an example).

MORE CARD-MAKING OPTIONS

There are many ways to embellish your handmade cards. Here are some of my favorites:

Stencils: Use small stencils of gardening tools, such as flowerpots and wheelbarrows, and "fill" them with hammered flowers.

Collages: Use woodland treasures, such as dried flowers, bits of dried grass, Spanish moss, fabrics, and paper on your cards. Use raffia to tie small bundles of treasures together, then glue them to the card.

Rubber stamps: If your calligraphy skills are somewhat lacking (as mine are), you can purchase rubber stamps to print just about anything you want to convey from *Happy Birthday* to *Congratulations.* Your hammered images, combined with a classy script from a stamp, will make your cards look very professional.

Lining the Envelope

*T*he best, most expensive cards come with envelopes that are as beautiful as the cards themselves. You can create your own classy envelopes easily and inexpensively, using the images from your hammered art. (See the lined envelope in the Rose Card photo on page 135.)

1. Use a thin, but absorbent paper, such as mulberry paper, which you can find in a craft store. (This takes the images of most plants better than rice paper.) Cut the paper so that it fits the inside front of the envelope, just underneath the glue to the bottom of the inside front.

2. Hammer bits and pieces of leaves and petals onto the paper to make an overall design.

3. Take a piece of double-sided tape and place it along the bottom edge of the liner paper.

4. Carefully slip the liner into the envelope and press the paper into place.

5. Put another strip of tape along the top edge and press this into place just underneath the strip of envelope glue.

~

Once you have an image that pleases you for a liner paper, you can use it over and over again by scanning it into the computer and printing it

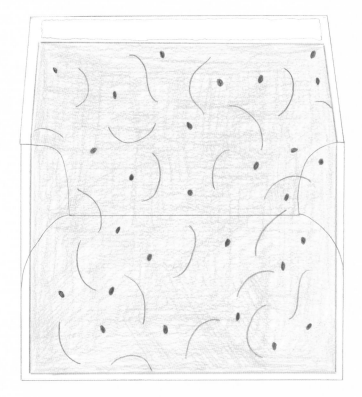

out on a thin paper, such as tracing paper, before you glue the original to the inside of the envelope. You might have to experiment a little to get the desired colors on the thin paper. Don't forget that you can enlarge or reduce the size of your image for special effects.

Rose Card

Roses are a symbol of love often used on Valentine's Day. You can, of course, use other pink or red flowers for your Valentine cards—pink or red primroses, for example, work well. This design also makes a wonderful birthday or Mother's Day card.

Piece of mordanted fabric, about 4 x 6 inches (for one card)

Plain greeting cards (type of paper does not matter)

Mini rose or full-size rose petals, sepals, and stem

Several small rose leaves

Pinking shears

Craft glue

Ribbon (optional)

Hammer

Iron

Scissors

1. Cut pieces of treated fabric slightly larger than your card. Make certain that the fabric is well pressed, with no wrinkles.

2. Design the card by placing the leaves and petals on the fabric in a pleasing way. You could position mini rose petals in a circle on the fabric, or overlap three petals from a full-sized rose, having them point upward. Hammer any petals, sepals, leaves, and stems onto the fabric.

3. Heat-set the images with the iron.

4. Cut your decorated fabric the same size as your card, using pinking shears so the fabric will not ravel.

5. Use craft glue to adhere the fabric to the front of the card. Make a border with matching or complementing ribbon, if desired.

~

Cost: $ Time: about 15 minutes each Difficulty: easy

Accordion-fold Book

Instead of a card, make a small book to give as a gift. When my niece had her last ballet recital, I made her a small accordion book, using images of flowers that I had made into ballerinas (see the Ballet Class Picture on page 74). I photocopied the images so they would not fade.

Sheet of heavy paper, 16 x 5½ inches (Make sure it's not too stiff to fold easily; I used watercolor paper.)

Extra flowers for decorating cover (I used mini rose petals and rose leaves.)

Sheet of colored paper (I used light purple to match the ballerina clothes.)

One color copy sheet of four images, with each image centered on a rectangle no larger than 3½ x 4 inches (I had four ballerinas.)

Piece of fabric or paper, 4 x 5½ inches (optional)

Piece of fusible vinyl (optional)

Piece of fusible webbing (optional)

Glue stick

1 yard of ⅛-inch ribbon

Pencil

Ruler

Small charms (optional)

Scissors

1. Cut the heavy paper to exactly 16 x 5½ inches. Fold it in half so the short ends meet and your piece measures 8 x 5½ inches.

2. Fold in half again, taking the short end back to the fold so that when you unfold it you have four "pages" measuring 4 x 5½ inches.

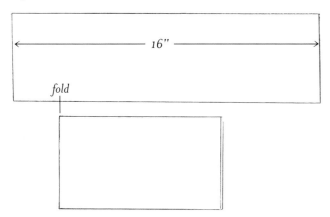

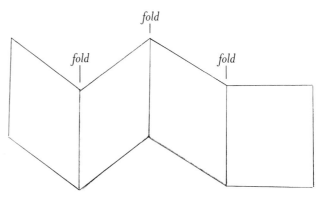

THE ART AND CRAFT OF POUNDING FLOWERS

3. Cut or tear the colored paper to get four pages, each 3¾ x 5 inches. Cut each copied image into a small page measuring 3½ x 4 inches.

4. Starting on the first inside page (leave the cover for now), glue one colored paper to the accordion book. Next glue an image on top of this, centering it on the colored paper. Repeat on the three other pages.

5. If desired, decorate the 4 x 5½-inch fabric or paper and glue it to the front cover. I typed "The Ballet Class" into my computer and printed it in pink ink onto a piece of thin cotton (see "Duplicating the Images" on pages 29–30). I decorated the printed fabric by hammering a few pink rose petals below the title. I then cut a piece of fusible webbing and a piece of fusible vinyl the size of the cover. Following the manufacturer's directions, I adhered the vinyl to the top of the fabric and the webbing to the back, then ironed the entire thing to the front of the book. The result is a very professional looking cover that won't smear or run.

6. Turn the book so the back cover is face up. Use a pencil to mark a dot at the center of the back fold. Measure 12 inches of ribbon (but do not cut it) and glue it to the fold at your mark, leaving a 12-inch tail. Continue running the ribbon to the second and third folds, gluing it at the center of each fold, then at the center of the front cover fold, leaving another 12-inch tail, as shown in the illustration. Close the book and tie the ribbon ends together on the right-hand side of the book. If you like, tie or glue a small charm to the ends of the ribbons.

~

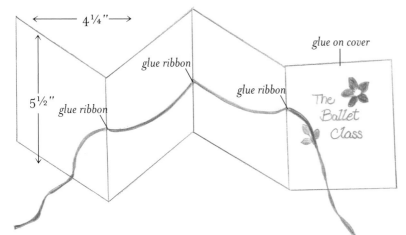

Cost: $ Time: about 1 hour Difficulty: moderate

Make It Simple: To save time, just hammer the images across a length of watercolor paper (spacing to fit within each page), fold into an accordian book, and you're done.

"DRAWING" WITH PETALS AND LEAVES

Don't limit your floral crafting to ballerina figures—you can use petals and leaves to "draw" almost anything! Here are some suggestions:

Letters: Most letters are made from a combination of straight lines and circles, both of which are readily available in flower shapes.

   Chrysanthemums have straight petals that are just right for making lines, while mini rose blossoms provide perfect circles. Begin by practicing the easy letters, such as capital M or L. Choose petals of similar length and position them carefully on paper or fabric and hammer. Lower-case letters such as "a" or "e" can be made by hammering a single round mini rose petal, then adding a "tail" made with a straight chrysanthemum petal. Let your imagination run wild and

soon you'll be seeing the entire alphabet in petals and leaves! Then you'll be ready to make projects such as a plaque with a child's name written out in petals, set off with a border of hammered flowers and ferns.

Butterflies and dragonflies: Balloon flower petals, split in half, are particularly good for making butterflies. Hammer one petal half, leave a small space for the butterfly body, then hammer the other petal half on the opposite side. For a dragonfly, layer petals on top of one another to give the illusion of two pairs of wings. The body can be made from a piece of root or a brown stem, or by cutting a piece from a dark leaf or petal. Create antennae by hammering slender stalks or stamens from the plant of your choice.

Calling Cards and Gift Tags

Business cards and old-fashioned calling cards can be enhanced with a tiny flower or fern image on the side. You can either create a single, stunning card and have this duplicated by the hundreds at a printing store, or you can simply take ready-made cards and put your own decorations on them one by one. Either way, you'll create a card that is uniquely yours.

Gift tags can also be embellished with hammered art. These can be as simple as a plain white card impressed with a single image or as elaborate as the gift itself. Consider some of the following:

- Make a round clay ornament with a floral impression to tie onto the top of a gift box and write "To:" and "From:" on the back with a metal-tipped pen before you bake it.

- Purchase a rubber stamp that says "To:" and "From:" and stamp this onto a small white card. Then embellish the card with a small hammered image (just be certain that your plant material will hammer successfully onto the card—choose a card stock that does not have a shiny or glazed surface). Try lobelia, larkspur, small zinnia, mini rose, or asparagus fern for a festive look.

- Hammer your favorite images onto a tightly woven cotton that you can write on as well. Cut into appropriate sizes and glue to the fronts of small cards.

Christmas Wreath Card

*T*his elegant Christmas card is very easy to create—you just hammer fern pieces onto a pre-made card and add a bow.

Several pieces of asparagus fern
Blank greeting card or watercolor card (or make your own from watercolor paper)
Pencil and compass
Plastic wrap
Removable tape (optional)
About 14 inches of ¼-inch red ribbon (per card)
Glue
Envelope
Hammer
Scissors

1. Cut the asparagus fern so that you have two dozen or so individual pieces that vary in length from ½ inch to 1½ inches.

2. If you are making your own cards, cut them from watercolor paper, then fold in half either horizontally or vertically. (If you are cutting your own cards, be sure that you can get envelopes to match the size of your cards before you make them!)

3. Use the pencil and compass to trace a perfect circle on the front of the card (or use the bottom of a drinking glass or small bowl). Be sure to keep your pencil lines light.

4. Open up the card so that you are hammering on a single layer of paper. Place a piece of the

fern on the pencil line, but at a slight angle so that when you're done, the pieces will look as though they are intertwined. Place a piece of plastic wrap over the fern piece and hammer.

place fern pieces over the circle

THE ART AND CRAFT OF POUNDING FLOWERS

5. Continue to place pieces of fern on the card, using your circle as a guide so that your wreath will look even when you're done. Once you get the hang of it, you'll probably be able to place a couple of pieces and hammer them at one time. Just be sure that they don't slip as you work with them. *Note:* If you use tape to secure the plant to the paper, be sure that you use removable tape. Regular tape will not pull off the paper cleanly.

6. When you have completed the wreath, tie a small red ribbon bow and glue it to the bottom of the wreath. If you're really ambitious, you can cut pieces of ribbon and glue them to the card to give the impression of the ribbon weaving in and out of the wreath.

~

<small>COST: $ TIME: about 15 minutes each DIFFICULTY: easy</small>

glue ribbon here   *glue ribbon here*

Make It Simple: Take your finished card to a copy store and have them run color copies on card stock. To add a bit of a 3-D look, put individual bows on each card when you get home. You can purchase ready-made tiny bows in a craft store if you don't want to tie your own.

Cloth Christmas Ornaments

Ferns and leaves, hammered onto white cloth and framed with small, red ornament frames, make a great decoration for your own holiday tree and a perfect gift for a hostess or friend. (These make great gift-box toppers, too.) The frames are quite inexpensive, but look richer when decorated with the hammered image and tied with a raffia bow.

3 pieces of white fabric* a few inches larger than the picture frames

Small red plastic or metallic picture frames, 3 inches to a side or smaller

3 leaves or ferns that fit inside the frames

Craft glue or hot glue gun

Cardboard

Hammer

* *You can use unmordanted fabric, though the ferns will stay green longer on mordanted fabric—but even then, not for an entire year.*

1. Hammer the images on the three pieces of fabric, making sure the images will fit inside the picture frames. Then cut the fabric to fit the frames.

2. Glue each piece of decorated fabric to a cardboard frame back, then push it into frame, gluing in place, if needed.

~

Cost: $ Time: about 10 minutes each
Difficulty: easy

Clay Christmas Ornaments

This is the perfect craft to do with children during those exciting days preceding the holidays. Plus, the ornaments make nice gifts for friends and family.

Small (2 ounce) package of white, red, or green polymer clay
   (makes several ornaments)
Plastic wrap
Rolling pin
Small round cookie cutter, 1½ inches across
Narrow red or green ribbon, 18 inches long (for each ornament)
Small ferns, flowers, or leaves, no more than 1½ inches across
   (Christmas fern is especially appropriate.)
Toothpick or wooden skewer
Polymer clay glaze
Small paintbrush
Oven
Aluminum foil
Baking sheet

1. Cover your work surface with plastic wrap. Roll out the clay to a thickness of ¼ inch and cut out rounds with the cookie cutter.

2. Press (or gently hammer) ferns, flowers, or leaves into the clay rounds.

3. Use a toothpick or wooden skewer to poke a small hole in the top of the ornament to thread with ribbon for hanging. Do this before you bake the ornaments!

4. Cut a piece of aluminum foil to fit in the baking sheet. Place the clay rounds on the foil-lined sheet and bake at 275°F for 10 minutes or until hard.

5. Let the ornaments cool, then apply a coat of glaze with the paintbrush. When dry, put ribbon through the top hole. Tie a bow at the top and double knot it. Then, take the two ribbon ends and tie them together to form a big loop for hanging. *Note:* If you forget to poke a hole in the top, glue a magnet to the back and use as a refrigerator magnet instead of a tree ornament.

~

Cost: $ Time: about 30 minutes   Difficulty: easy

144   THE ART AND CRAFT OF POUNDING FLOWERS

Christmas Napkins

Decorated cloth napkins make a holiday table look festive. Because napkins need to be washed every time you use them, it's best to do this project by making a good hammered image, printing it on iron-on transfer paper, and ironing an image on each napkin.

White 16-inch square napkin, preferably all cotton
8½ x 11-inch piece of mordanted fabric
Asparagus fern
Iron-on transfer paper
2 yards of ¼-inch red satin ribbon per napkin
Color copier or printer
Sewing machine or needle and thread
Hammer
Iron

1. Wash, dry, and iron the napkins and set aside.

2. Take a small sprig of asparagus fern, about 1½ inches wide and 3 inches tall, and place it on a folded napkin to check out the size and design. Adjust, if necessary. Remember that an iron-on transfer will give you a mirror image. When you're pleased with your design, remove the fern from the napkin and hammer it onto the mordanted fabric.

3. Repeat this with several other pieces of fern, covering the piece of mordanted fabric. Be sure to leave ample margins on each side (for a finished 8½ x 11-inch sheet) and small spaces between the fern pieces.

4. Make iron-on transfers from this sheet of impressed cotton with a color copier or printer (see "Duplicating the Images" on pages 29–30).

5. Cut out the iron-on transfer images as precisely as possible, leaving little of the background paper. Then place one fern image on a napkin in the bottom right-hand corner. Iron the transfer onto the napkin, being careful not to scorch the napkin!

6. Sew the ribbon around the face of the napkin, ½ inch in from each edge.

~

Cost: $ Time: about an hour (to make 4 napkins)
Difficulty: moderate

Christmas Stocking

The simple lines of these ferns are set off by the rich red satin top, making this a stocking worthy of "hanging by the chimney with care." If you want this to be a functional stocking that will last for many years, hammer the fern onto cotton fabric first and then make iron-on transfers (see "Duplicating the Images" on pages 29–30).

½ yard of white linen or cotton, mordanted

Ferns (Asparagus fern and young, light green Boston fern work well; I used rabbit foot fern fronds on white linen.)

¼ yard of red felt

⅓ yard of ¼-inch red satin ribbon for hanging

Sewing machine and white thread

Glue

Paper

Pencil

Pins

Hammer

Iron

Scissors

1. Iron the mordanted cloth thoroughly until there are no wrinkles.

2. Draw a stocking shape 15 inches long and 7 inches wide, and 11 inches wide at the boot on a piece of paper. Cut out to use as a pattern.

3. Fold the mordanted fabric in half and use the paper pattern to cut out two stocking shapes.

4. Position the ferns in various places on one piece of stocking fabric. This will be the front of the stocking. When you are pleased with the design, hammer the ferns onto the fabric.

5. Heat-set the images with the iron.

6. Take the front, decorated piece and the undecorated back piece and place them right sides together. Pin the edges, then stitch along all edges of the stocking with a ½-inch seam, leaving the top open. Turn the stocking right side out.

7. Cut a piece of the red felt 7 inches wide x 3 inches long. Stitch the short ends together with a ½-inch seam, making a tubular cuff piece. Glue the bottom of the cuff to the top of the stocking, covering the raw edge of the stocking.

glue here

8. Fold the red satin ribbon in half, making a big loop. Sew the bottom of the loop to the top left-hand edge of the stocking cuff.

~

COST: $$ TIME: 1–1½ hours DIFFICULTY: moderate

Make It Simple: Buy a white cotton or felt stocking. Place a piece of foil or wax paper inside the stocking to keep pigments from going through and hammer the ferns in place. If the stocking does not have a cuff, cut one out of red felt and glue or stitch into place.

Decorative Wrappings

Hammered art is perfect for all the wrappings and trappings of celebrations. Make your own gift wrap or simply decorate ribbons to tie around solid-colored purchased wrapping paper. You can make small gift bags from paper or fabric, or decorate bags purchased at craft or card stores.

Gift Bags

Cloth or paper gift bags
Flowers, ferns, and leaves (I used a pansy.)
Ribbon to coordinate with the bag
Small square of fabric
Gift tag or card
Wax paper or aluminum foil
Hammer

1. Place the bag on a flat hammering surface. Slip a piece of wax paper or foil inside the bag to prevent the pigments from going through to the other side.

2. Position ferns, flowers, or leaves on the bag and hammer. You can decorate both sides or just one.

3. When you've filled the bag, tie it with a color-coordinated ribbon.

4. Make a gift tag by hammering a floral or leaf image onto a small square of fabric and then gluing it to a tag or card.

~

COST: $–$$ TIME: a few minutes DIFFICULTY: easy

Make It Simple: Make your impression on fabric, then cut out and glue it to the outside of a shiny paper bag. Or layer and glue pieces of fabric and colorful paper on the bag to make a collage.

Wrapping Paper and Ribbons

You can make your own unique and beautiful wrapping paper by hammering images onto absorbent paper. Unfortunately, inexpensive wrapping paper or shelf paper does not generally take images very well. Thicker paper, such as watercolor paper, is better for hammering, but is more difficult to use to wrap gifts. A good compromise is to buy large sheets of good-quality paper at a craft store. Look through the stacks to find papers that do not have a shiny finish and seem to be soft and absorbent. Mulberry paper, though thin, absorbs colors well and is excellent for making both gift wrap and colorful papers suitable for collage.

If you are wrapping something firm, such as a book, you can wait until the gift is wrapped with your special paper before you hammer your images, so you can position them in just the right places. Just be certain that the pigments won't go straight through the paper to your gift. If your gift does not lend itself to this, then wrap the gift with your chosen paper, making folds and creases where needed, and remove the paper. Use the folds and creases as a guide for placing your images. Hammer the images onto the paper, then rewrap it around your gift.

An overall print, such as that made by layering ferns or leaves, is a good choice on gift wrap paper. You can add interest to the print with brightly colored petals, such as those from dianthus or lobelia. If your paper is very thin, first wrap the gift with white tissue paper, then wrap again with your finished wrapping paper.

ENHANCING RIBBON

Plain white ribbon can be beautifully enhanced with floral impressions. The impressions are not crisp and perfect, because the pigments tend to bleed a bit on the ribbon, but the overall effect is quite lovely. You must use small flowers that fit on the ribbon. Good choices include violas, lobelia, pink oxalis, mini roses, and pieces of asparagus fern.

You can also make sheets of iron-on transfers with small blossoms and use the transfers for decorating ribbon as you need it. Simply cut out the images and iron them onto the ribbon for a colorful decoration.

< *Phlox, viola, lobelia, and ferns were used to decorate this paper.*

More Info

PLANT GUIDE
QUICK REFERENCE CHART

Plant Guide

When you begin to use plants for hammering, your perspective on the plant world will change. You will become more acutely aware of flowers, colors, and shapes, always wondering how they will look as hammered art. Unfortunately, not all plants hammer with equal beauty. I have spent countless hours experimenting with various petals, stems, and leaves on a wide variety of fabrics and papers; I've used any number of combinations of cover materials to determine which plants are suitable for hammering. This guide is an accounting of my trials, errors, and successes.

Please don't limit your art to the plants I've listed. After all, I am only one person living in one part of the United States, using the plant materials that are available to me. Try whatever you have available to you, and try the plants at different times of the growing season, since pigments and moisture levels change as plants age.

My descriptions here of the hammering techniques and results are, for most entries, brief. Please refer to Chapter 2 for step-by-step techniques for pretreating fabrics, hammering, duplicating, and enhancing the images. The chart on pages 175–182 contains more detailed information about how the plant images transferred on various fabrics and paper. Please note that all the fabrics I used were mordanted with alum.

ASPARAGUS FERN
Asparagus setaceus

Asparagus fern is neither an edible asparagus nor a fern, but is a wonderfully soft, frilly plant with dark green needles along thin, wiry stems. It is one of the best of all plants to hammer because it transfers beautifully to most materials. It is particularly good to use during the winter holidays, since the finely textured leaves look like miniature Christmas trees or evergreen branches. If you plan to use this plant to make multiple crafts, purchase a plant in early fall so that it will grow enough by the holidays to give you plenty of material.

How to Grow: In most parts of the country asparagus fern is grown as a houseplant, though in frost-free areas it is grown outdoors with great success. Although the plant will withstand light frost, severe cold will kill it. If planting outdoors, choose a spot that has well-drained soil and receives filtered sunlight. If growing indoors, place the fern in a large pot set in a place that receives indirect sunlight. Prune out old, dead stalks

and feed once a month with a general houseplant fertilizer. Even though the plant can go long periods without water, once asparagus fern is established, its growth will be faster and more luxuriant if it is watered regularly.

How to Hammer: Using a pair of small, sharp scissors, clip off small branches of the plant, approximately 1½ to 2 inches long. It's best if you can use two pieces that are still attached (in a V or L shape). Use larger pieces for larger projects, such as the Christmas stocking on pages 146–147. Fern leaves are easy to use. They take little prep work and can be placed directly on paper or fabric and then hammered. To get the most detail from hammering, though, choose pieces that are not too full.

ASTER
Aster spp.

In nature, most asters are perennials that usually bloom in late summer or autumn in a wonderful array of purples and lavenders. Fortunately, florists have cultivated some species to grow in commercial

greenhouses so we can buy cut stems throughout the year. Florists' asters usually consist of a thick stalk covered with numerous small purple flowers with yellow centers. Like all members of the daisy family, each individual blossom is actually made up of ray flowers (ones that look like petals) and disc flowers (yellow ones that make up the center of the blossom).

The results of hammering the entire blossom are not always satisfactory, since the centers are large and filled with moisture. However, if you remove the center, you can get a very nice impression from the small ray flowers.

How to Treat: As a cut stem, asters last a week or so. To extend their lives, place stems in a vase of water and place in the refrigerator until ready to use. Since you're using only the blossoms, remove the bottom portion of the stem.

How to Hammer: Scotch tape is the trick! Clip off a blossom and place it on the fabric. Take several small pieces of tape and use them to adhere the purple ray flowers (these look like petals) to the fabric. If the small blossom has an abundance of ray flowers, you might want to remove some of these before you tape it down. When the flowers are secure, take a pair of small, sharp scissors and clip the center out of the blossom. Place the fabric on a paper

towel (double paper towels for silk) on top of a wooden board. Lay the blossom on the fabric, cover with a piece of plastic wrap, and hammer well.

BALLOON FLOWER
Platycodon grandiflorus

The common name of this easy-to-grow perennial is balloon flower, due to the rounded shape of its buds, which resemble balloons. Although the plant comes in pink, white, and blue, the blue flowers are superior for hammering; the veins in the petals are distinct and make perfect "butterfly wings" for your fantasy creations.

How to Grow: It takes three to four years for balloon flowers to become well established. Plant in full sun or where they will receive light afternoon shade. Water regularly, and feed with a slow-release fertilizer. When you cut stems to bring indoors, cut the flowers in late afternoon or early evening and put the stems in deep water overnight. The next day, recut the stems and strip off the lower leaves.

Pick spent flowers to extend the blooming season.

Balloon flower plants die back completely in fall and do not reappear until late spring. Be certain to mark the spot in your garden so you won't inadvertently dig into the roots or crowns before the new stems appear above ground.

How to Hammer: Balloon flowers open out into slightly cupped, star-shaped blossoms measuring almost 2 inches across. Because they are cupped, they will not lie flat unless you take a pair of small scissors and slit the petals almost to the center. Cut them just until the blossom lies flat. Remove the hard green parts to which the blossom is attached, then place on fabric or paper. Put a paper towel under the fabric and on top of the blossom and hammer thoroughly.

BEE BALM
Monarda didyma

This is another one of the best plants I tested for hammering. The configuration of the flowers produced an unusual image, and I was astonished at the clear, bright red color that transferred so easily from the petals.

Bee balm is a perennial native to the eastern United States and is used both as an herb to make tea and as a garden plant to attract hummingbirds. The plant has scarlet flowers surrounded by reddish bracts, and grows 24 to 36 inches tall, while the blossoms usually measure from ½ to almost 3 inches across. Many cultivars have been developed that vary in color from pink to purple.

How to Grow: Bee balm prefers moist soils and should not be allowed to dry out. It needs full sun for good blooming and rich soil for sturdy growth. Plants spread very quickly where happy, so site them in a wild garden or away from less vigorous perennials. Its leaves are often chewed on by garden pests, but blossoms are usually unaffected. You can extend the blooming time by as long as 2 months by picking off spent blossoms.

How to Hammer: You must take bee balm flowers apart before you hammer them. You will need to hammer individual petals and bracts to give the impression of the entire plant. The bracts themselves transfer beautifully, providing great vein details, and give depth and interest to the impression. Only a few of the tubular flowers need to be hammered to create a wonderful design. Use paper towels underneath the fabric and on top

of the plant material. Taping the bracts keeps them perfectly still and results in a more detailed impression.

BEGONIA, WAX
Begonia semperflorens

This popular plant blooms profusely throughout the warm months in most climates. It is originally from Brazil, but is now one of our more common summer bedding plants. The leaves are bright green or bronze, while the blossoms are white (not suitable for hammering), pink, or red. Although begonias don't offer a stunning transfer, they are useful for specialty projects. The petals from pink begonias are the perfect size and color for the face of a "flower fairy" (see pages 122–124) It's also a useful plant for adding a touch of pink or red to a design.

How to Grow: This is a great shade plant and should be grown in rich, well-drained garden soil. Given sufficient moisture, begonias also grow in full sun in most areas of the country. They are heavy feeders and respond well to

regular applications of fertilizer throughout the growing season. Begonias are intolerant of cold temperatures and should not be planted until all danger of freezing or cool temperatures has passed in spring. In mild climates, they will thrive for years and can grow quite large.

How to Hammer: Clip off the stem and place the blossom face down on the fabric or paper. Allow the yellow center to remain. Be sure to use ample padding underneath the fabric.

BLACKBERRY LILY
Belamcanda chinensis

This tall (3- to 4-foot), graceful plant puts forth sprays of small, orange blossoms covered with dark red speckles. Each blossom lasts only a single day, but new blossoms open throughout the blooming period, which usually lasts for weeks. The common name comes from the seed pods, which are round and split open to show small, shiny black seeds that resemble blackberries.

How to Grow: Plant rhizomes in fall to a depth of 1 inch in a spot where they will receive full sun to partial shade. Blackberry lilies need rich, well-drained porous soil and regular watering, and are particularly attractive when planted in groups. If grown in ideal conditions this plant spreads nicely, forming handsome clumps of flowers and foliage.

How to Hammer: Remove the blossom from the stem and place it face down on your fabric, making sure that the petals are well separated. Put a paper towel underneath the fabric and on top of the plant, then hammer thoroughly.

BUTTER DAISY
Leucanthemum paludosum

This small annual grows only 6 inches tall and, in many regions, reseeds prolifically, coming up the following year in the most unexpected places. The plants, however, stay neat and compact and rarely become invasive. Though not spectacularly showy, butter daisy offers reliable bloom throughout the summer and into fall. The transfers fade rapidly, so the plant has limited usefulness for hammering, but it is one of the best

flowers to use for decorating polymer clay projects.

How to Grow: Start seeds indoors 4 weeks before the last frost, or sow outside once the soil has warmed. Butter daisy prefers full sun, tolerates heat and humidity, and is somewhat drought tolerant. The blossoms fade and drop off, so deadheading is not necessary. This plant will flower well into fall where temperatures are moderate.

How to Hammer: The petals need to be taped down and the center removed, as described for aster (see page 155). Put a paper towel under your fabric and on top of the flower, then hammer thoroughly.

CARROT TOPS
Daucus carota

The beautiful bright-green leaves of carrots are often still on the vegetables you buy at the market, even during the winter months. This is good news for hammering enthusiasts because carrot tops make very satisfactory transfers.

How to Treat: You can simply leave the tops on the carrots, put the vegetables in a plastic bag, and store

them in the crisper drawer of the refrigerator; or you can remove the tops and place them in a glass of water—a method that keeps them looking fresh longer. For maximum life, place the carrot tops in a glass or vase of water and place in the refrigerator.

How to Hammer: Carrot tops need little prep work. As you place them on the material, be sure to spread out the individual leaves and leaf parts so they do not overlap. There is almost always a "fold" in the leaf toward the bottom of the stem—cut this out so you can transfer a single layer. Be sure to use the leaves with the greatest number of indentations, because these give you the most interesting transfers. Place paper towels under your fabric and over the carrot tops for the best transfer (if you're hammering on silk, use double paper towels underneath and on top). Hammer well, being certain to press evenly all over the greens, particularly on the edges.

CALADIUM
Caladium bicolor
If I had to choose a single plant to hammer, it would probably be caladium. It transfers in beautiful, minute detail, requires no prep work, transfers to all fabrics, and the images last a long time without fading. It is, in fact, a perfect hammering plant.

Caladiums are tender

plants, intolerant of frost. They are grown for their large arrow-shaped leaves that show bands and spots of white, red, green, silver, bronze, and rose. Smaller-leaved varieties are also available. Caladium grows about 2 feet tall, though dwarf varieties have been developed.

How to Grow: Caladiums grow from tubers and can be set out in pots or in the ground. They prefer rich soil, high humidity, and warm temperatures. They do best when temperatures do not drop below 60°F at night and are above 70°F during the day.

In spring, plant tubers in pots indoors in March, or plant outdoors when the weather has warmed considerably and there is no threat of frost. Plant tubers with knobby side up, so the tops are even with the soil surface. Feed lightly throughout the growing season, particularly if growing in containers. Pot caladiums in a soilless potting mix. For best results moisten the mix in a large bucket before filling pots and planting tubers.

When the weather cools,

bring in potted caladium plants or, dig up the tubers growing in the ground and store them for the winter. Knock off excess soil and dry in semishade for 1 to 2 weeks, then store in dry peat moss at 50°F to 60°F.

How to Hammer: Just pick a leaf at the stem, place it on a piece of fabric (with a paper towel under the fabric), and hammer. Be certain to hammer thoroughly, getting each part of the leaf. Because this hammers so easily, you can use a thin piece of fabric as the cover material, and get an extra image for the same amount of hammering.

CHRYSANTHEMUM
Chrysanthemum morifolium

Traditional fall bedding plants, chrysanthemums are also popular indoor potted plants with flowers that are good for cutting. There is tremendous variation in the flower forms, but the florists' chrysanthemum is generally a semidouble flower that comes in white (not suitable for hammering), yellow, bronze, red, pink, purple, and orange.

How to Grow: Keep potted plants in a cool, sunny window and keep soil evenly moist. Pinch off the dead flowers as they fade. Either discard florist chrysanthemums when they are finished blooming or plant them in the garden. Depending on where you live, florist chrysanthemums may or may not bloom again in the garden. In the north, the flowers often are killed by frost in fall before they have a chance to open.

In the garden, plant in well-drained, moist soil that has been amended with generous amounts of organic matter. Set out young plants in early spring and feed with a flower fertilizer two or three times during the growing season.

How to Treat: If you purchase cut flowers, remove the lower foliage and hammer the ends of the stems, particularly if they are tough and woody. Place the stems in a deep container of cool water up to the blossoms for three hours, then remove and place in vase. Be sure to keep the water clean. Keep in a cool spot until ready to hammer.

How to Hammer: Like all daisy-type flowers, you will have to take the chrysanthemum apart and reassemble it to make your impression. If you hammer the entire flower head, you will end up with one big blob of color. Carefully pull individual petals (actually ray flowers) out from the center. Try to choose petals that are approximately the same length. Place these on the fabric with the ends touching in the center. For a 3-D look, alternate long and short petals. Except for silk, these can be taped to the fabric before hammering, though be sure to use a paper towel underneath. Silk requires a paper towel beneath the fabric and on top of the plant.

CLEOME
Cleome hassleriana

This annual with unusual, but striking, flowers is enormously useful if you are interested in creating flower figure impressions (fairies, ballerinas, etc.) with hammered art. Cleome's stamens are very long, bright pink, and slender, and make perfect "arms" and "legs" for flower figures. The petals are about ½ inch long, and different cultivars offer white, pink, or pink-purple flowers. The plants grow 3 to 4 or more feet tall and the flowers sit along the tops of the stems.

How to Grow: A native of South America, cleome is a summer annual that needs to be planted in sun to partial shade. It does not tolerate frost and grows best in rich, deep soil with generous amounts of water and regular applications of fertilizer, particularly early in the growing season. Sow seeds in the garden after danger of frost has passed. Cleome self-sows readily.

How to Hammer: You will have to take the flowers apart and reassemble them to make your impressions. To hammer an entire flower, remove the stamens and hammer the petals in a circle or as a "side view," using three petals. Then place the stamens over the petals and hammer.

COLEUS
Solenostemon scutellarioides

Grown for its colorful foliage, coleus has enjoyed a revival of interest over the past decade. New cultivars, particularly those with tiny leaves, have been developed, extending the usefulness of this old-fashioned favorite. The leaves are often brilliantly colored and include shades of chartreuse, yellow, salmon, orange, red, pink, green, maroon, and purple. One leaf will often feature many colors.

How to Grow: This is a terrific plant for partial

shade, though many cultivars also tolerate full sun as well. A rule of thumb is that the more colorful the leaf, the more sun it can tolerate. Plant coleus in the spring in beds, hanging baskets, or containers. It thrives in rich, moist soil with good drainage. Water regularly throughout the growing season. The plants can be easily propagated by rooting the leaves in water or a mix of half perlite, half vermiculite, and replanting once a good root system is established.

How to Hammer: One of the easiest plants to hammer, coleus leaves need no prep work and can simply be placed on fabric and hammered. Put a paper towel underneath the fabric and on top of the leaf and hammer thoroughly, making sure to hit all edges evenly. Because there are so many different colors of coleus leaves, be sure to test out your particular leaves on fabric scraps before you hammer them onto a project. Although the colors will fade on almost all fabrics, the patterns they create remain attractive.

COREOPSIS

Coreopsis lanceolata
This is one of the few yellow flowers that provides a long-lasting, bright yellow transfer (the other of note is marigold). Annual coreopsis, *C. tinctoria*, also transfers beautifully, though the plant itself is not as widely

grown and may be difficult to find. *Coreopsis verticillata,* threadleaf coreopsis, is another perennial with bright lemon-yellow blossoms that transfer well. Coreopsis is a native perennial wildflower with a wonderful profusion of yellow or red-yellow blossoms.

How to Grow: Coreopsis does well in full sun with moderate watering. Plant in the spring in moderately rich soil with good drainage and divide every three or four years, as needed, to keep the plant vigorous. Both *C. lanceolata* and *C. tinctoria* grow easily from seed sown directly into the garden. This is a temperate plant and does not do well in extremely cold or hot regions. To generate as many flowers as possible, deadhead spent blooms.

How to Hammer: Take the petals off and hammer them one at a time to obtain the cleanest transfer, though it is possible to place the entire blossom on a surface and pound the center lightly and the petals more firmly. Be certain to hammer the very ends of the petals, which are notched and give a nice shape to the

impression. Place paper towels underneath your fabric and on top of the plant, or use Scotch tape to hold the petals in place.

COSMOS

Cosmos bipinnatus

This tall plant with large pink, dark-pink, and white daisy-like flowers is an easy-to-grow summer annual. The petals are notched on the ends and transfer brilliantly. The leaves, which are airy and fernlike, also transfer well.

How to Grow: Start from seed indoors in late winter, then transplant into the garden when all danger of frost has passed, or sow seeds directly outdoors in beds where they will receive full sun. Cosmos blooms best in moderately rich, well-drained soil and often reseeds abundantly. Supply plants with moderate amounts of water throughout the growing season and clip off spent blooms to stimulate further flowering. Although this species can grow as tall as 8 feet, shorter strains grow only 3 to 5 feet tall.

How to Hammer: You can hammer the entire plant at

once, for a nice 3-D effect. Place plenty of padding underneath your fabric to absorb the fluid from the center and the petals. Place the blossom face-down on your fabric and cover with a paper towel or plastic wrap. Hammer the center very gently, gradually increasing the pressure. Hammer the petals firmly until they have all transferred.

DAHLIA

Dahlia spp.

Early fall brings a peak of dahlia blooms. Spanish explorers found them growing in Mexican gardens, where they were not only revered for their beauty, but much appreciated for their edible tubers, whose high sugar content helped treat diabetics before the discovery of insulin. There are many different kinds of dahlia flowers, including anemone forms (with cupped petals) and cactus forms, which have long, narrow, spinelike petals.

How to Grow: Dahlias need full sun or very light shade and ample water during dry summer months. The plants benefit from rich topsoil and frequent applications of compost, well-rotted manure, or fertilizer, which helps prevent the leaves from turning yellow.

Plant tubers in spring after all danger of frost has passed, setting them 12 inches deep in holes between 1 and 3 feet apart, depending on the size of the tuber. Fill in the holes gradually with soil as the tubers sprout. After the first fall frost, dig up the tubers and allow them to dry in the sun for a few hours. Cover with sawdust or peat moss and store indoors in a cool, dry place until spring.

How to Hammer: Most dahlias should be hammered by pulling individual petals from the center and hammering in a circular pattern. Place a paper towel underneath the fabric and on top of the plant before hammering.

DIANTHUS
Dianthus spp.

Dianthus, sweet William, pinks, and carnations all belong to the genus *Dianthus*. These plants have been grown for many centuries, as evidenced by designs of

carnations found on tiles dating back to the fifteenth century. The ancient Greeks considered this the "flower of flowers" (the genus name actually means divine flower).

Dianthus are characterized by petals that are notched or jagged on the ends. The name "pink" actually comes from the word "pinct" meaning scalloped. To pink (as with pinking shears) means to cut with a jagged edge. Colors range in the pink and red tones, although there are many white cultivars available and you can now purchase florist's carnations in every color of the rainbow. Most dianthus foliage is gray or gray-green.

How to Grow: Dianthus bedding plants are either short-lived perennials or biennials and are often treated as annuals. Perennial selections grow in almost all climates. Place in a sunny spot in very well-drained natural or slightly alkaline soil. Dianthus thrives in relatively cool weather and blooming is most prolific in spring. To extend the blooming period, be sure to pick spent flowers. Even perennial types are considered short-lived and should be divided every 2 to 3 years to retain vigor. Propagate by division.

How to Hammer: Both the blossom and the leaves are suitable for hammering. Pull the petals apart and

hammer separately. Although in nature the petals overlap, it's best to hammer them so that they do not touch, to show the shape and configuration of each petal. If the petal color is light, experiment by overlapping the petals, getting deeper tones where they touch. Place paper towels underneath the fabric and on top of the plant before you hammer.

DILL
Anethum graveolens

Soft, feathery leaves make dill ideal for hammering onto fabric; the plant also releases a wonderful smell as it is crushed. Grown in the garden, dill often reaches 3 to 4 feet in height.

How to Grow: Dill grows easily from seeds sown directly into the garden. In warmer regions, plants grow better in spring than during the hot summer, since they quickly go to seed in warm weather. Sow seeds in well-tilled, rich garden soil that drains well, and thin seedlings to about 18 inches apart. Successive sowings will assure you of plenty of dill for the entire growing season.

How to Hammer: With very little effort, you can "comb" the leaves so each one lies separately on the material and impresses individually, with very satisfying results. Pick small pieces of leaves, either young yellow-green or older, darker green ones. Place paper towels under the fabric and over the plant before hammering.

DOGWOOD, PINK
Cornus florida 'Pink Flame'

Spring brings clouds of white and pink dogwood blossoms to many parts of the country. Unfortunately, though the traditional white dogwood blossom is undeniably beautiful, it is useless for making impressions. But the trees with pink bracts (dogwood "blossoms" are actually composed of four large bracts rather than petals) offer wonderful materials for hammering, and trees with nearly red blossoms are even better.

How to Grow: Flowering dogwood is native to the eastern United States from New England south to Florida. It grows 20 to 30 feet tall, has attractive horizontal branching, and leaves that turn a rich, deep red in fall. Plant young trees in deep, fertile soil where they receive full sun or filtered shade. Dogwoods will not bloom in heavy shade.

How to Hammer: The deeper the pink or red tones of the bracts, the more pigment present and the better the transfer you will get. No matter what shade it is, though, you'll obtain the best results by gently separating the bracts and hammering them without the hard center part of the cluster. The bracts hammer best when they are a little wilted because they'll lie flatter than bracts that are fresh off the tree. The leaves also transfer beautifully to fabric.

Separate the bracts, then reassemble them on your fabric, making sure the centers are touching and the bracts make a cross pattern as they do in nature. Taping the bracts to the fabric sometimes gives you a more detailed transfer but is not necessary. Use a paper towel under the fabric and cover the bracts with plastic wrap or wax paper before hammering.

FERNS

Various species; see list below
Ferns are perfect plants to use in a variety of hammered art projects. They are available throughout much of the year, either as garden plants or houseplants, and generally transfer beauti-

fully, though older fern fronds give a fainter transfer than younger, fleshier ones. If they are too fleshy, however, you'll get only a mass of green for your efforts. Here are the ferns I have worked with:

CHRISTMAS FERN
(Polystichum acrostichoides)

LADY FERN
(Athyrium filix-femina)

MAIDENHAIR FERN
(Adiantum pedatum)

NEW YORK FERN
(Thelypteris noveboracensis)

RABBIT FOOT FERN
(Davallia fejeensis)

ROYAL FERN
(Osmunda regalis)

How to Grow: Although there are dozens of different species of ferns, they all generally prefer shady, moist conditions. Be sure the soil has plenty of organic matter and the plants are supplied with sufficient moisture during the growing season.

How to Hammer: One of the easiest plants to hammer, ferns can just be placed on fabric or paper and pounded. On paper or leather, you will generally get a "negative" impression, meaning that the pigment

appears as an outline of the frond, rather than on the inside of the image. Because fronds of varying ages give different intensities of transfers, ferns are perfect for a "layered" look. For a crisp transfer, tape the fronds down. For an impressionistic look, hammer quickly and don't worry about getting each tiny detail. Unless the fronds are very old or very new, place a paper towel underneath the fabric and plastic wrap on top of the fern. For new growth, use a paper towel under the fabric and on top of the fern. For old growth, place the fabric directly on the hammering surface, with no padding underneath, and use plastic wrap on top of the fern.

GERBER DAISY (TRANSVAAL DAISY)

Gerbera jamesonii

The bright, colorful blossoms of the gerberas are favorites of the floral industry. They can be found throughout the year, on potted plants and cut flowers. Although the native species was orange-red, the blossoms now come in a wide array of colors.

How to Grow: In coastal or tropical areas, gerberas can be grown as perennials. In cooler regions, they are grown as annuals. The plant requires very good drainage and rich soil, and needs to be fed frequently during the active growing season. Although plants bloom at any time during the year, the greatest profusion of blossoms come in early summer and fall.

How to Treat: If you purchase cut flowers, wait until the blooms are fully opened, then make a 1-inch slit in the bottom of the stem. Place in water and keep in a cool place. Because the blossom has so many petals on it, a single flower offers enough material to make several impressions.

How to Hammer: You will have to take the daisy-like flower apart and reassemble it. If you hammer the entire flower head, you end up with one big blob of color. Carefully pull individual petals out from the center. Try to choose petals that are approximately the same length. Place these on the fabric with the ends touching in the center. For a 3-D look, alternate long and short petals. You can tape the petals to the fabric before hammering, though be sure to use a paper towel underneath. If you are using silk, do not tape the petals. Put a paper towel under the silk and a paper towel on top of the petals before hammering.

GRAPE, MUSCADINE
Vitis rotundifolia

Muscadine grapes, native to the southern United States, produce finely veined leaves that are excellent for hammering. The grape skin, however, only gives a squirt of color, so it is best to use only the leaves.

How to Grow: Muscadines and other grapes are vines that need support. If you are only interested in growing a vine for shade (or to produce leaves for hammering) the requirements are minimal. You will need to provide some type of support—an arbor, trellis, or stakes—and you will need to prune the vine each year to keep it from becoming a tangled mass. Otherwise, grapevines need little effort on your part. But if you want fruit from your grapevine as well as foliage, the vine must receive plenty of sunlight, must be pruned at the right time in the right way (consult a gardening book), and must be given plenty of nutrients if the soil is deficient.

How to Hammer: Hammering the leaves is easy. Simply place a leaf vein-side down on the fabric or paper and hammer thoroughly. If the leaf has begun to dry out, do not use any paper towel padding—place the fabric or paper directly on the wooden hammering surface and cover the leaf with plastic wrap. The new, bronzy leaves offer a beautiful pink color and are easier to hammer than the older leaves. The veins transfer beautifully and in great detail.

HOLLYHOCK, MALLOW
Malva sylvestris

Although many plants from this genus transfer well, this dwarf cultivar is the most useful because of its compact size. I used a mallow with other small summer blooms to create the summer floral pattern used on the Bedroom Set on pages 56–58. It has a pleasant shape and color, and transfers predictably well. But don't be afraid to try other, larger hollyhocks as well (the single, rather than the double, flower types are easier to work with).

How to Grow: Most varieties of hollyhocks grow on flowering stems that tower over the rest of the garden—sometimes as tall as 9 feet—and must be staked. Mallow, however, is compact and able to stand on its own. Hollyhocks can be annuals, biennials, or perennials, depending on the species chosen. They need full sun and regular watering, and prefer soil that is heavy and moist, but not too rich, since they have a tendency to develop rust disease.

If grown in a temperate climate, hollyhocks can be cut back after the first flowering, and if watered and fed, will produce a second crop of flowers. After flowering has stopped, cut the stems to the ground and mulch the perennial species.

How to Hammer: Miniature hollyhock blossoms can be hammered as a whole because their centers are not too hard or fleshy. The small, green sepals, or centers, give an added dimension to the image. Put a paper towel under the fabric and on top of the blossoms and hammer thoroughly.

IMPATIENS
Impatiens walleriana
As beautiful as they are common, impatiens fill shady garden beds in many areas of the country. This plant produces abundant blossoms in a wide variety of colors, including white (not useful for hammering purposes), pink, red, and salmon.

How to Grow: Although impatiens are perennial in their growth cycle, in most regions they are treated as annuals, because they are extremely sensitive to frost. Impatiens bloom best when grown in a semishaded spot and receive plenty of water. In warm climates, they wilt in the heat of the midday sun if not sufficiently irrigated. The plants perform best with regular feedings throughout the growing season, and often reseed or can be propagated by stem cuttings placed in water. Although there are strains with miniature and double flowers, the single, old-fashioned cultivars are best for hammering.

How to Hammer: Although the thin-petaled blossoms and leaves both hammer well, the stems are thick and fleshy and do not make good impressions. Remove the back spur of the blossom, if present, and place the flower face down. Be sure to have good padding (at least one layer of paper towel) beneath the fabric and a paper towel over the plant to absorb the moisture.

IRIS, DUTCH
Iris spp.

Though iris is traditionally a late-spring plant, Dutch iris is also a florist's favorite that can be found year-round. This is a plant that you'll absolutely have to take apart and reassemble to get a good impression. Choose the brightest, most colorful iris blossoms you can find, and the results will be well worth the trouble.

How to Grow: In the fall, plant bulbs about 4 inches deep, 3 to 4 inches apart. If you're gardening in a hot and sunny region, place them where they will receive afternoon sun; otherwise, plant them in full sun. (Iris can also be grown in a pot.) Water regularly during the active growth season.

How to Treat: If you purchase cut flowers, place the stems in a tall container filled with water so that most of the stem is submerged. Leave for a few hours, then put the iris into a vase or other container. Sometimes flowers will open successively up the stem. Remove each spent blossom after it flowers. Irises can also be cut

when still in bud and the flowers will continue to open indoors.

How to Hammer: It's difficult to reconstruct the iris exactly, but you can definitely get an iris look-alike impression. With care, you should be able to get two impressions from a single blossom. For each impression, you will need three pieces of standards (upright petals) and two pieces of the falls (long curving petals with yellow down the center). Because the yellow part is fleshy and full of moisture, you'll get a better impression if you remove this. You will also need two pieces of the recurved petals.

Carefully pull one standard out from the center and cut this down the center into two pieces. Pull one more standard out and cut it the same way. Gently pull out one of the falls from the center of the blossom and split it down the center as well, then remove the fleshy yellow parts along the edge. Pull out one of the recurved petals from the center and cut this in half, lengthwise.

To reassemble on your fabric, place a paper towel underneath the fabric, then place the three standards in the center, but do not allow them to overlap. Place the two falls, pointing upward, on either side of the standards, then position the recurved petals, pointing downward, adjacent to the

falls. This positioning gives you a very good likeness of the iris.

Split the leaves in half lengthwise. To give depth to your impression, place one leaf "behind" the blossom. Do not actually overlap the plant parts; instead, cut the leaf just below and just above the petal it goes "behind."

Split the stem in half, wipe off any extra moisture or sap from the stem, and hammer it underneath the blossom.

IRONWEED
Vernonia noveboracensis

One of the most beautiful of all autumn roadside plants is tall and stately ironweed. The small, starry blossoms of this perennial are a bright rosy-purple and appear on open clusters at the ends of the flowering stems. Leaves are dark green, and both blossoms and leaves give excellent transfers. Ironweed can grow 7 to 8 feet tall and is best used at the back of the garden border.

How to Grow: A field flower, ironweed is not demanding in its needs and grows readily in both moist and dry soils. It needs full

sun to bloom well and to develop stems strong enough to stand without staking.

How to Hammer: To get an effective image, you need to hammer only a small portion of the flowers that occur on a single flowering stem. Remove individual blossoms and seed heads from the flowering stem and hammer a portion of the stem, including several forks and branches. Take individual flowers and place them along the hammered stem and hammer. Hammer as many blossoms onto the stem as desired, but don't make the images too crowded.

IVY, ENGLISH
Hedera helix

You must use tender, new leaves to get a good transfer from ivy, because older leaves produce a waxy covering that makes it almost impossible to release the pigments. So, even though you might have acres of ivy growing outside your house, you'll have to purchase a potted plant to get fresh, new growth during the cold months of the year. An alternative, of course, is to plan ahead and pot up some ivy during the summer months.

There are many different ivy cultivars available, some of which have interestingly shaped leaves. Unfortunately, the best veining is in the older leaves, which do not hammer well.

How to Grow: Ivy is very easy to grow, indoors and out, and thrives in a variety of garden conditions. Place in a sunny window and keep the soil evenly moist. Outdoors, plant in well-drained soil, in sun or shade.

How to Hammer: Use fairly new, young leaves, but not the tiniest ones, which are too soft to transfer well. Place paper towels underneath the fabric and on top of the leaves before you hammer. Be sure to hammer evenly all over each leaf.

KUDZU
Pueraria lobata

Getting a beautiful hammered image from kudzu was a great surprise. Not only does the leaf transfer beautifully, but the blossoms, which appear in early fall, make a stunning transfer, as well. Kudzu is actually an invasive weed that was introduced to this country

in 1876. It now overtakes abandoned and waste areas in the southern United States. The lobed leaves come in threes and appear on vines that can grow up to 1 foot a day. Do not plant kudzu, no matter how beautiful the hammered images are. You can always get it from roadsides.

How to Hammer: The blossoms appear in clusters and must be taken apart for the best images. Each cluster of flowers supplies enough blooms to make several full impressions. Remove the larger blossoms from the central stem, but leave the short stems that attach the blossoms to the main flowering stem. Keep the small terminal buds.

Hammer the stem and terminal buds first, retaining the natural, graceful curve of the stem. Then begin to reassemble the larger blooms. Carefully split individual flowers into two parts, removing the inner filaments and anthers. Place these at the ends of the small flower stems and hammer each part separately. The blooms in the cluster will be in different stages of maturity, so be sure that you include some of each, placing them on your design as they occurred naturally on the stem. It will be easier to do this if you use two blossoms—one to take apart to hammer and one to look at as an example. Leaves need to be placed vein side down for the best transfer.

Be sure to hammer them thoroughly, because it's difficult to get an even transfer.

LARKSPUR
Consolida ajacis

This annual comes in shades of bright blue, light blue, white, and pink. For hammering purposes, the brighter the color, the better the transfer. Larkspur's blooming season is directly correlated to the climate in which it is grown—hot weather causes the blooms to fade rapidly. In cooler regions, you will find larkspur blooming well into September. The plants grow 2 to 4 feet tall and produce stunning stalks of flowers and lacy, fernlike leaves. Some strains produce flowering stalks 4 to 5 feet tall with large blossoms.

How to Grow: Larkspur grows well in moist, rich, well-drained, and slightly acidic soil in full sun. Sow seeds in fall for early summer blooms, or sow indoors 6 to 8 weeks before setting seedlings out in spring. Supply with plenty of moisture but also provide good air circulation, because the plants are subject to fungus

and mildew. When planting in the garden, always sow in clusters for the most impact.

How to Hammer: It can be difficult to release the intense blue color of larkspur, particularly when it's late in the bloom season. So place your fabric directly on the wooden hammering surface and cover the plant with plastic wrap. If you do not get a clear image, put a paper towel underneath the fabric and adjust the padding thickness until you get satisfactory results.

You can hammer larkspur in different ways: For a front view, clip off the long spur and remove the center parts, being careful to keep the petals attached. Place on the fabric, face up toward you, and hammer well. For a side view, leave the spur, remove a couple of the petals, and hammer. Often you'll get not only the blue of the petals but a wonderful blue-green in the center as well.

LOBELIA
Lobelia erinus 'Crystal Palace'

Lobelia makes my top ten list—its intense blue color and interesting blossom shape make it ideal for creating stunning impressions. It is easy to hammer, gives you a dependable transfer that does not fade, and hammers equally well on paper and fabric. It is my favorite flower for hammering.

How to Grow: Lobelia is an annual bedding plant that needs cool temperatures and will not withstand hot and humid summers. Plant in early spring in rich, well-drained soil and fertilize once a month.

How to Hammer: Carefully pinch off blossoms and remove the tiny green sepals at the base of the tubular flowers. Place face down on your fabric and try to separate the three lower petals and the two small upper ones to give a more interesting design. Place a paper towel underneath the fabric and on top of the flower and hammer.

LOROPETALUM
Loropetalum chinense

A fairly recent introduction to the Western horticultural world, loropetalum has long been prized in its native China. It is a wonderful tender shrub with soft leaves that turn from pink

to dark green to maroon, and all colors in between. It grows 10 to 15 feet tall in the southern United States and produces white to greenish flowers. The cultivar 'Ruburm' has startlingly bright pink flowers, well suited for hammering. The blossoms are composed of four narrow, twisting petals.

How to Grow: Plant in partial shade or full sun in rich, well-drained neutral or slightly acidic soil. Although it will survive periods of drought, loropetalum performs better with regular watering. The shrub responds well to pruning, although its open, sprawling growth habit is also nice. If desired, you can prune lower branches to create a tree shape.

How to Hammer: Although the flowers make interesting transfers, it is the leaves—in their subtle variations of pinks and greens—that are the real hammering stars. This is one of the best leaves to use for good color and excellent detail on watercolor paper. Be sure to hammer the leaf vein side down. Unless the leaf is very young and fleshy, a single layer of paper towel underneath the fabric and on top of the leaf is sufficient.

MAPLE, JAPANESE
Acer palmatum
The small, intricately detailed leaves of Japanese maples are great specimens

for hammering. From the early spring growth into the rich green tones of summer, and through the brilliant reds and oranges of fall, these leaves offer a variety of color and texture unrivaled by any other plant. In addition, they are just the right size for many hammered art projects. There are countless varieties and cultivars of Japanese maples, and the trees range in size from bonsai to a towering 30 feet. They can be straight-trunked, vaselike, or weeping.

How to Grow: Japanese maples need good drainage and lots of water. The colors are best when the trees are grown in filtered sun or partial shade. If grown in full sun, the leaves often burn; and if grown in full shade, the trees do not grow well and autumn colors are subdued. They are light feeders, requiring only a bit of fertilizer in early spring; too much fertilizer makes them weak and spindly.

How to Hammer: The hammering technique varies depending on the growth cycle of the plant. When hammering young leaves, place paper towels

both underneath the fabric and on top of the leaf. When hammering older leaves, particularly in autumn when they have begun to dry out, you will get a better transfer if you place the fabric directly onto the wooden surface and cover the leaf with plastic wrap rather than a paper towel. If the leaf is very dry, it will not transfer at all. Experiment with various thicknesses of paper towels to get the right absorbency.

MARIGOLD
Tagetes patula

Marigolds have been a staple in annual beds for decades and were especially popular in the Victorian era. The bright flowers transfer beautifully, giving lasting impressions in shades of yellow and orange.

French marigolds grow in all regions of the country and are considered easy to grow because they suffer little damage from pests and disease. They have a long blooming season, a distinctive odor in the leaves, and a profusion of blossoms.

How to Grow: Provide full sun and moderately rich

soil, and marigolds will reward you with an abundance of blooms. There are many different cultivars, including single, double, and semidouble flowers in shades of yellow, orange, and red. Marigolds grow well in beds and borders as well as in containers, and are easily started indoors from seeds sown in early spring. But wait until all danger of frost has passed before you plant them outdoors. Keep spent blooms picked off, and feed every 4 to 6 weeks during the growing season.

How to Hammer: Remove several petals from the flower and hammer them separately. One double or semi-double marigold blossom provides enough petals for many impressions. The leaves also transfer well. Place paper towels underneath the fabric and either a paper towel, tape, or plastic wrap on top of the flower or leaf and hammer well.

MOSS PINK, CREEPING PHLOX

Phlox subulata

This old-fashioned favorite carpets rock gardens and

tumbles over stone walls in early spring, bringing a big splash of color to the spring garden. The short and narrow evergreen leaves create a creeping mat about 6 inches tall. Different cultivars offer flowers ranging in color from bright pink to lavender to blue-and-white. Moss pink offers one of the greatest surprises for hammering because the bright pink flowers turn bluish-purple almost immediately when hammered onto paper or fabric.

How to Grow: Moss pink spreads quickly when grown in the right conditions—friable soil, but not too rich, and moderate watering, particularly during the blooming season.

How to Hammer: Moss pink needs little prep work. Just carefully clip off a bit of the long tube at the base of the flower, place paper towels underneath the fabric and on top of the flower, and hammer a few times. It transfers quickly and easily, and a thorough hammering will give deeper tones and crisper edges. You can use plastic wrap or wax paper on top to better see what you're doing, but if the blossoms are very young or you are using a thin fabric, such as silk, a paper towel will give you a cleaner transfer.

NANDINA

Nandina domestica

A great plant for hammering! Nandina is evergreen

in warm regions and marginally hardy in cooler climates. Although the species plants grow 6 to 8 feet tall, many new dwarf cultivars grow much shorter and produce colorful leaves throughout most of the growing season. Neither the white clusters of spring flowers nor the bundles of bright red winter berries are useful for hammering, but both make this an unusually attractive garden plant. The leaves and stems are best for hammering. New leaves are bronzy colored and turn bright green during summer months, crimson in winter.

How to Grow: Nandina is tolerant of a wide variety of growing conditions, including drought, sun, or shade, though it does require well-drained soil. The shrub loses its leaves when temperatures drop below 10°F and suffers stem damage when it gets colder than 5°F, but the plant generally recovers quickly. For best growth, place in rich soil and provide with regular water. Prune with hand pruners, not hedge shears, and cut back to a tuft of leaves. To prune

tall and sprawling plants, cut back the stem to ⅓ its height and allow it to fill out.

How to Hammer: Young and summer green leaves hammer fairly easily and give nice, crisp lines and good color. The stem hammers beautifully to create a thin green line that is useful for many projects. Fall and winter leaves transfer nicely, though the color isn't easy to extract. For very young leaves, use paper towels below the leaf and above it for padding. As the leaves begin to age and lose moisture, take some of the padding away. Place fall and winter leaves vein-side down and hammer hard with the fabric or paper directly on the wooden hammering surface.

NIGELLA, LOVE-IN-A-MIST

Nigella damascena

Love-in-a-mist is grown for its beautiful seedpods as well as its unusual flowers. The blossoms are blue, white, or pink. The brighter colored blossoms transfer best. Leaves, even those found directly beneath the blossom, are finely dissected, looking somewhat like those of Queen Anne's lace.

How to Grow: This annual is best grown from seeds sown directly into the garden in early spring, as soon as the ground can be worked. An alternative is to plant indoors in peat pots 4 to 6 weeks before the last frost. Plants flower once, then set seeds, so make a series of sowings for continual bloom. Nigella needs full sun and excellent drainage. The plants should be fed monthly, but watered only when the soil dries out. They reseed abundantly when grown in a suitable location.

How to Hammer: Fortunately, you can hammer both the blossom and the first layer of leaves all at the same time, resulting in a beautiful 3-D effect. Clip the blossom and first set of leaves off the stem before hammering. Use a paper towel beneath the fabric and on top of the plant.

OXALIS, PINK
Oxalis adenophylla

This is one of many plants casually referred to as "shamrock." The plant blooms in spring with bell-

shaped pink flowers about 1 inch wide on stalks 4 inches to 6 inches tall. They differ in color intensity, so choose the brightest blossoms for making impressions.

How to Grow: Pink oxalis is easy to grow in many regions and is somewhat invasive in areas where the leaves remain evergreen and the blooming period lasts for many months. In the North, grow it as a houseplant. It thrives in sun and well-drained soils with moderate fertility, and is a good plant for rock gardens or for edging.

How to Hammer: Pink oxalis needs little prep work. The basal tube and tiny green sepals can be snipped back a little for a cleaner transfer, but other than that, just put it down and hammer. Place a paper towel underneath the fabric and on top of the plant before hammering. If you need precise positioning, tape the blossom down and then hammer. The leaves transfer well, but fade within a few months.

PANSY
Viola wittrockiana
Pansies, extremely variable in color, provide an interesting array of impressions. Similar to violas, pansy petals transfer beautifully, showing detailed venation. However, avoid plants with really dark "faces" because these transfers do not work

well. I found that the best transfers were created from small- to medium-sized blue or purple blossoms with distinct venation.

How to Grow: Pansies are annuals that grow in most regions of the country. In warmer climates they can be planted in the fall and allowed to develop a good root system during the winter. Plant in rich, well-drained soil and feed with a slow-release fertilizer at the beginning of the blooming season. In spring, they begin to bloom early and put on a show until the weather turns hot. To get more blooms, pick faded blossoms off the plants.

How to Hammer: For the best transfer, put a paper towel over the hammering surface, lay down your fabric, then place the blossom face down on the fabric. Using cellophane tape, secure the petals to the fabric. When all the petals are taped, carefully snip off the green sepals and gently remove them, taking care to keep the petals in the same position. Cover the petals with plastic wrap or, if the petals seem

fleshy, cover with a paper towel, and hammer. Be thorough and make sure you catch all the edges.

PERIWINKLE, ROSE
Catharanthus roseus

This tender perennial with bright-pink, red, or white flowers is usually grown as an annual during the summer months. It is drought resistant and blooms even during the hottest weather. As with most garden flowers, the brighter the blossoms, the better the image transfer, so avoid using white cultivars—even those with a bright central "eye."

How to Grow: Rose periwinkles thrive in full sun and moist, well-drained soil. They benefit from periodic feeding during the most active flowering period. They don't do well in heavy, clay soils.

How to Hammer: The petals are connected by a long, narrow tube. Clip the tube but keep the petals attached. Put a paper towel under your fabric, then place the blossom face down on the fabric. Put a paper towel on top of the blossom and hammer.

PETUNIA

Petunia x hybrida

Although the newest wave of petunias ('Purple Wave' and 'Pink Wave') have become enormously popular recently, petunias have always been a favorite bedding plant. The blossoms are funnel-shaped and many cultivars have beautiful veining, making them nice for transfers. An astonishing number of cultivars is available, but the single, unruffled flowers are the ones best suited for hammering.

How to Grow: Petunias need full sun and excellent drainage, and can be grown in containers as well as in garden beds. Allow the soil to dry out between watering and feed regularly during the growing season. Smaller-blossomed varieties take summer heat better than those with giant flowers.

Seeds should be started indoors 8 to 10 weeks before the last frost. Do not cover the seeds—they need light to germinate. Press them into the soil with the bottom of a glass. Petunia seedlings are so readily available that you may choose to purchase plants rather than to try to start your own.

How to Hammer: You must split petunia blossoms in half, hammering a side view rather than using the full flower. This technique will create a nice variation from the more common round shapes of other hammered impressions. Use a paper towel underneath the fabric and either plastic wrap or paper towels on top of the blossoms and hammer thoroughly.

PHLOX

Phlox paniculata

Phlox is a beautiful, 3- to 4-foot tall perennial that blooms in midsummer. There are many cultivars but the bright-pink blooms (even though they come out purple) are the best choices for hammering. Each individual flower measures about 1 inch across and the flowers are in clusters about 8 inches across.

How to Grow: Phlox needs full sun and rich, well-drained soil. Because the plants are susceptible to powdery mildew, it's important they be placed where there is good air circulation, and that they are watered at their base instead of with an overhead sprinkler. Plant in spring or, in warmer regions, in the fall. Although phlox grows and blooms in many regions of the country, plants do best where the summers are not excessively hot and humid.

How to Hammer: Each blossom is slightly tubular. Remove the bottom tube, so that the petals spread out evenly. Put a paper towel under your fabric and a paper towel, plastic wrap, or tape on top of the petals before hammering.

PHLOX, WILD BLUE

Phlox divaricata

This early blooming wildflower offers a pale-blue shade. It fades relatively quickly though, and is best used as an iron-on transfer (see pages 29–31) or as a pattern for embroidery or painting (see pages 33–34). The blossom color varies, with some blossoms so light they are almost white, while others are a nice, deep lavender-blue. Choose the darker blossoms for hammering.

How to Grow: In warmer climates wild blue phlox has semi-evergreen leaves and flowering stalks that are about 1 foot high. It is a woodland plant and should be grown in shade or filtered sunlight in moist, rich soil.

How to Hammer: For a cleaner transfer, snip off the tubular base of the blossom before hammering. The fabric can be placed directly on the hammering surface, unless you're using a thin silk, in which case put a paper towel under the fabric. You can use either plastic wrap or a paper towel on top of the plant. The leaves also transfer nicely.

PINCUSHION FLOWER

Scabiosa atropurpurea

Scabiosa's common name comes from the profusion of yellow or white stamens grouped in the center of its flower clusters, like pins in a cushion. A wonderful, prolific bloomer that grows 1 to 3 feet tall, the plant looks great among other small summer flowers.

Although pincushion flowers come in blue, purple, pink, and white, I like the images I get from the unusual-shaped blue flowers the best.

How to Grow: This annual can be easily started from seed, either indoors several weeks before the last frost, or outside, once danger of frost has passed. It needs full sun and prefers rich, well-drained soil. Water moderately throughout the season, though take care to keep standing water off the foliage, because it doesn't like soggy conditions.

How to Hammer: Pincushion flowers need little prep work—simply pick the blossom off the stem, place it face down on your fabric (with paper towels under the fabric), then place paper towels over the flower and hammer. Hammer the petals first, using firm pressure, then hammer the center, starting very gently, and increasing pressure as needed.

PLUMBAGO
Ceratostigma plumbaginoides

The blue flowers of plumbago make nice impressions, but they will not be very intense. This plant is actually not a true plumbago (a sprawling shrub), but is a low-growing groundcover, only reaching a height of 12 to 18 inches. Plants can be vigorous spreaders and are best used as groundcovers under shrubs.

How to Grow: Plant in full sun or partial shade in loose, friable soil and provide plenty of water during the growing season. To be most effective as a groundcover, set small plants over a wide area and allow to grow and fill in. In autumn, the leaves turn a nice red.

How to Hammer: This is an easy flower to hammer, needing no prep work. Just put a paper towel underneath your fabric and on top of the blossom, and hammer.

PRIMROSE, COMMON
Primula vulgaris

The bright colors of primrose blossoms make them wonderful plants to hammer. They have clusters of flowers that come in vibrant tones of orange, pink, rose, red, purple, or blue.

How to Grow: Place potted plants, available from florists, in a bright window and supply with plenty of water. If you keep the plant in a cool place, the flowers will last longer, but remember to remove spent flowers. While florists' primroses usually are grown as annuals, garden centers offer common primroses that make fine perennials. Plant them in partial shade and rich, evenly moist soil.

How to Hammer: With a pair of scissors, clip out the center funnel part of the blossom, but don't cut so deeply that the petals separate. Place a paper towel underneath the fabric and another on top of the plant parts, and hammer well.

QUEEN ANNE'S LACE
Daucus carota

Although this is a terribly invasive weed in many regions, the blossoms have such an unusual configuration that it's well worth growing a few carefully controlled plants. In regions where it does not outgrow its welcome, it is a beautiful plant to include in the garden. It grows 4 to 5 feet tall and produces an abundance of lacy flower umbels and finely cut, fern-like leaves.

How to Grow: Queen Anne's Lace is a biennial that is easily grown from seed sown directly in the garden. The plant blooms during the second season, though in warm regions, flowers will form in summer on plants grown from seeds planted the previous fall. If you live in a region where this plant is invasive, be certain to clip off the flowering heads before they set seed.

How to Hammer: Instead of the flowers use the beautiful lacy leaves just underneath the flowering head. Pick a blossom that is past its prime and has begun to curl upward but has not yet dried out. Clip off the ends of the blossom stems, leaving the short green stalks and the leaves, which form a whorled pattern. Place this face down on your material and cover the plant with a piece of plastic wrap so you can see what you are hammering. Hammer gently, increasing pressure as the transfer comes through. Be sure to leave plenty of spaces between the short stems and leaves, even if you have to remove some of the stems. The impression will be all green, but the pattern it makes will look wonderful.

REDBUD
Cercis canadensis

Although the showiest part of the redbud tree is the

early spring flowers, it is not these pink-purple blooms that are best for hammering—it's the new heart-shaped leaves. They transfer in stunning detail, showing (on some fabrics) not only individual veins, but even shading around the veins. New leaf growth has a wonderful bronzy look while on the branch. This often hammers out as pink.

How to Grow: Redbud trees grow quickly and reach a height of 25 to 35 feet at maturity. Plants seed so readily redbuds are considered an invasive weed in some areas. Cultivars include 'Alba,' with white flowers, and 'Forest Pansy,' which has leaves that are pink-purple. Redbuds grow best in sandy, well-drained soils in full sun, though 'Forest Pansy' needs partial shade.

How to Hammer: Place your fabric directly on the wooden hammering surface, put down the leaf, cover it with a paper towel, and hammer. If the leaves are very young and fleshy, put a paper towel underneath the fabric. If they are older and drier and the pigment is slow to flow, try a piece of plastic wrap over the leaf instead of a paper towel.

ROSE, MINIATURE
Rosa spp.

Although a summer garden supplies you with countless rose blossoms for pounding, you can also use miniature

potted roses during winter months for the same purpose. The miniature roses are, in many ways, better for this craft because they are smaller. Both the leaves and blossoms transfer well. Experiment with any roses that are accessible to you, even florists' roses.

How to Grow: Indoors, grow in good potting soil and place in a window that receives bright sunlight. During the active growing season, keep the plant at room temperature and feed every two weeks. Like all roses, even miniatures need a period of cold and rest. During fall and winter months, keep plants at temperatures below 45°F and keep the soil barely moist. Resume watering and feeding in early spring as growth begins again.

How to Hammer: You will have to take rose flowers apart and reassemble them to make your impressions. If you hammer the entire flower head, you will end up with one big blob of color. Carefully pull individual petals out from the center. Choose petals that are approximately the same length and place these on

the fabric with the ends touching in the center. For a 3-D look, alternate long and short petals. Except when using silk, these can be taped to the fabric before hammering, though be sure to use a paper towel underneath. (Silk needs the absorbency of a paper towel beneath the fabric and on top of the plant.)

ROSE OF SHARON
Hibiscus syriacus

There are numerous species of hibiscus, all of which transfer a little differently. The plants with larger blossoms are a bit difficult to use because of their size, though many will transfer well. Larger blossoms are suitable for a large pattern or a project such as a shawl, where you have a wide expanse of fabric to work with. Simple blossoms, rather than double or ruffled, are much easier to hammer.

How to Grow: Rose of Sharon is a deciduous shrub or small tree. Its growing needs are minimal—it is partially drought tolerant and does not need overly rich soil. As with many flowers and shrubs, it will

grow in partial shade but will not bloom well unless it gets enough sunlight. To get the greatest amount of bloom, prune back the previous season's growth in late winter.

The leaves have three lobes and drop in fall without coloring. The blossoms, which somewhat resemble hollyhock flowers, are usually single, measuring 2½ to 3 inches across.

How to Hammer: Do not try to hammer blossoms that have begun to dry on the edges; these parts have lost pigmentation and will not transfer. You can hammer rose of Sharon in a circle after you remove the large center stamen and pistil. Pull the petals off one by one, making sure to keep the dark-red splotch at the inner end of the petal. Hammer the petals separately either in a circular pattern or with three petals pointing upward, as in a side view. Use paper towels beneath the fabric and on top of the petals.

SASSAFRAS
Sassafras albidum

Native to the eastern United States, this tree has

the distinguishing characteristic of producing three different leaf shapes on the same branch. The leaves can be either entire (without lobes), with one lobe (like a mitten), or three lobes. It's nice to have the three different leaf shapes right on hand to use in various designs. The tree can grow to a height of 60 feet. It has red-brown, furrowed bark and leaves that turn orange and red in fall. These hammer nicely, and also release a citrusy smell when you hammer them.

How to Grow: Sassafras is a good tree to use in a naturalized garden; it thrives in partial shade and well-drained, slightly acidic soil. Look for nursery-grown seedlings at your local garden center.

How to Hammer: Put a paper towel under your fabric, place the leaves on the fabric vein-side down, and put a piece of plastic wrap on top of the leaf. Hammer thoroughly.

SOURWOOD

Oxydendrum arboreum

Sourwood, native to the eastern part of the country, is one of the first trees to turn orange, red, or dark purple in the fall; the leaves also hammer beautifully. The tree produces long, graceful clusters of fragrant, bell-shaped white flowers in summer, but these are not suitable for hammering.

How to Grow: Sourwoods are considered easy to grow, though they prefer slightly acidic, well drained soil and will not tolerate high levels of urban pollution. They are somewhat drought tolerant, but prefer regular watering. The tree will grow in partial shade, but will flower better and produce stronger fall color if grown in full sun.

How to Hammer: Leaves should be placed vein side down on fabric, with paper towels under the fabric and on top of the leaves. If a leaf has begun to dry, place the fabric directly onto the wooden hammering surface and cover the leaf with plastic wrap instead of a paper towel. To get the best image, try taping the leaf to the fabric. Be careful to select leaves that are not crisp or brown on the edges, because these will not transfer pigments.

STOKES ASTER

Stokesia laevis

Stokes aster is a perennial wildflower native to the southeastern United States. This species has been the object of extensive breeding, however, and there are now many cultivars available. Plants bloom for about four

weeks in summer. Each flower measures 2 to 3 inches across and is made up of outer, large, deeply notched ray flowers and a circle of much smaller disc flowers, similar to a daisy.

How to Grow: Plant in well-drained, rich soil at the front of a bed or border. Stokes asters do best in filtered sunlight and cannot tolerate soggy conditions during winter. In northern regions, protect them from the cold with a deep layer of mulch. To propagate, divide established plants in spring.

How to Hammer: Remove the outer, notched petals and hammer these one at a time, recreating the circular shape of the flower. Place a paper towel underneath the fabric and cover the petals with plastic wrap or a paper towel. Don't try to hammer entire flowers at once or you will get a murky puddle.

SUMAC, STAGHORN

Rhus typhina

Distinguished for its brilliant fall colors and its interesting clusters of dark red berries, staghorn sumac is appreciated both as a roadside decoration and a

garden plant. The leaves turn bright red in fall and make nice transfers.

How to Grow: Numerous species of sumacs do well in moist, well-drained soil. Staghorn sumac grows as a shrub or small tree and is considered quite hardy and even slightly invasive because its roots send out many suckers. It can get up to 15 feet tall.

How to Hammer: The fall leaves hammer out a dull red on almost all fabrics. They must be hammered vein side down. Sometimes the ends of the leaves, even though they don't look like it, will be dry and will not release colors, leaving you with a half-leaf image. So use the freshest, brightest leaves possible. Place the fabric or paper directly onto the wooden hammering surface and cover the leaf with plastic wrap.

SWEETGUM

Liquidambar styraciflua

The star-shaped leaves of sweetgum trees resemble maple leaves. In fall they turn yellow, purple, or red. The descriptive genus name, *Liquidambar*, refers to the golden sap of the tree.

How to Grow: Plant in full sun or partial shade in slightly acidic soil. Sweetgums tolerate salt spray, but suffer from high winds. The species is native from Connecticut west to Missouri and south to Mexico.

How to Hammer: Pick fresh and colorful leaves and place vein-side down on fabric that sits directly on the wooden hammering surface. Cover the leaf with plastic wrap. If the leaves are still full of moisture, place a paper towel beneath the fabric and/or on top of the leaf to see if you can get a crisper transfer.

SWITCH GRASS
Panicum virgatum

When this beautiful grass is blooming and just before it goes to seed, it makes a great hammering plant. The stalks are long and slender, and the immature seeds

transfer a nutty brown color. But once the seeds have begun to dry out, they do not transfer nearly as well.

How to Grow: Switch grass is native to the prairie states and needs full sun and relatively dry conditions. There are cultivars that are bigger and more stunning in the landscape, but for hammering purposes, the roadside variety does just fine.

How to Hammer: The blossoms tend to grow on one side of the stem, so you might have to do some rearranging to get a more even transfer, or you might want to make this a part of your design and aim for a "wind swept" look. Switch grass is one of the easiest plants to hammer, and even though it does not offer bright colors or intricate details, it does create an airy, beautiful pattern. Put a paper towel under your fabric, then arrange the grass in a pleasing design. Cover with another paper towel and hammer thoroughly.

VERBENA
Verbena × hybrida
The small, brilliantly colored blossoms of verbena make this one of the most satisfactory of all plants for hammering. New cultivars bear even brighter colors than before and this plant is now available in blue, purple, lavender, red, and pink. It grows low to the ground—only 6 to 8 inches

tall—and is used as a groundcover or in containers and hanging baskets.

How to Grow: Verbenas need full sun, rich, well-drained soil and moderate amounts of water. They are heavy feeders and should be treated to full-strength fertilizer frequently during the growing season. Be certain to place plants where they get plenty of air circulation, for they are susceptible to mildew. Although verbenas tolerate heat, flowering is reduced during extremely hot weather.

You can start verbena from seed in the spring, but the seedlings are subject to damping off, a condition caused by too much moisture that kills them. Nursery-grown plants are much easier to start with. Plant when all danger of frost has passed.

How to Hammer: Verbena is an easy plant to hammer. Simply take an individual blossom and pinch off the tubular end. Place a paper towel underneath your fabric and either plastic wrap or a paper towel on top of the blossom, then hammer thoroughly. This is a great plant to use with young

children—the flowers are small and transfer well, so success is almost guaranteed. Tape down a blossom and let your kids go at it.

VINCA
Vinca spp.

Vinca is an aggressive groundcover that can be quite invasive in wooded areas. Grow this plant with care, and keep it in check to prevent it from choking surrounding vegetation. The dark, shiny leaves are evergreen and the blue blossoms appear in spring. Some vinca impressions are stunningly beautiful with full, deep tones. Others fade out from the center, leaving only a rim of color, so you'll need to experiment with different plants.

How to Grow: Vincas need partial to full shade and moderate watering. *Vinca minor* is not as invasive as *V. major* and comes in cultivars that offer dark-blue flowers that are great for pounding. But transfers from both *V. major* and *V. minor* are unpredictable.

How to Hammer: Dry each blossom thoroughly, sticking the end of a paper towel down into the tubular flower to wick away any moisture. Then, clip off as much of the flower tube as you can, but still keep the petals attached. Be sure to use mordanted fabric and put paper towels underneath the fabric and on top of the plant material before hammering.

VIOLA
Viola cornuta

Violas were developed from a little English wildflower known as a Johnny-jump-up. The faces on this flower and the hundreds of cultivars developed from it have given rise to names such as Monkey Faces, Peeping Tom, and Three-Faces-in-a-Hood. Viola blossoms come in shades of violet, blue, and yellow. The cultivars with distinct veining make better hammered impressions than those with solid colors.

How to Grow: In mild regions, violas can be planted in the fall. They will bloom sporadically until early spring, then in profusion as the weather warms. In cooler areas, violas are an early spring plant and, where summers remain cool, can last throughout the hot months as well. Violas are heavy feeders and benefit from regular applications of a flower fertilizer. They bloom well in both sun and semishade, and need moderate moisture. In hot weather, flowers become smaller and the plants get long and leggy.

How to Hammer: To get a nice, clean transfer, you must remove the green stem and sepals from the back of the flower while keeping the small petals in position. Place the blossom face down on your fabric and carefully tape the petals down. (If you are hammering on watercolor paper, use removable tape.) Then, take small scissors and clip off the green parts, leaving only the petals. Hammer, then remove the tape.

VIRGINIA CREEPER
Parthenocissus quinquefolia

Also known as woodbine, Virginia creeper is a vine that grows enthusiastically in shady gardens and woods. The leaves are divided into five leaflets with serrated edges, and turn bright red, or sometimes a dull red, in fall.

How to Grow: Virginia creeper grows to 30 to 50 feet long and will clamor over the ground, or climb a wall, trellis, or other support. It is particularly useful as a groundcover on hillsides, where it helps control erosion. For best fall color, grow in partial sun in rich, moist soil. Set out young plants in spring and prune back for full, bushy growth. The leaves are tolerant to frost and will cling to the vine into mid- to late fall. This vine is deciduous, though, and the bright autumn leaves finally shrivel and drop.

How to Hammer: If the leaves have begun to dry out, place your fabric directly on a wooden hammering surface, then place the leaf on top of this—vein-side down—and cover with plastic wrap to force out as much pigment as possible. If leaves are still relatively fresh, try varying layers of paper towels under the fabric or on top of the leaf to get the best transfer.

WISTERIA
Wisteria sinensis

Although wisteria can become irritatingly invasive, the early spring cascade of flowers is so beautiful, it's easy to forgive its over-enthusiastic growth. The rich purple flowers are borne in graceful clusters, tapering to tiny buds at the ends. Although both purple and white flowered cultivars of this vine are available,

only the brightly colored purple blossoms are suitable for hammering.

How to Grow: If you plant wisteria in a garden, be sure that you prune diligently to keep it in bounds. There are tricks for stemming its growth, such as putting it in a large container that you bury in the ground, which essentially keeps the roots contained. There are cultivars that are less invasive and have deep-purple flowers, that are equally suitable for hammering.

How to Hammer: Although wisteria makes very nice impressions, it takes some work to take the flower clusters apart, and reassemble them on cloth or paper. Each cluster of flowers supplies enough blooms to make several full impressions. Start by putting a paper towel under your fabric or paper. Then remove the larger blossoms from the central stem, but leave the short stems that attach the blossoms to the main flowering stem. Keep the small terminal buds. Cover the stem and terminal buds with a paper towel and hammer them first, retaining the natural, graceful curve of the stem. Then begin to reassemble the larger blooms.

Carefully split individual flowers into two parts, removing the inner filaments and anthers. Place these at the ends of the small flower stems and hammer each part separately. The blooms in the cluster will be in different stages of maturity, so include some of each, placing them on your design as they occurred naturally on the stem. It's easier to do this if you use two blossoms—one to take apart to hammer and one to refer to as an example.

ZINNIA

Zinnia elegans and Z. haageana
Zinnias vary in size and blossom type and come in every color except blue,

giving you almost limitless variations for hammered images. The bright-orange blossoms of *Z. haageana* transfer very nicely, though the intense color may be a bit hard to fit into a design. Blooms of the more common *Z. elegans*, of which there are numerous cultivars, also transfer well, and most zinnia blossoms offer enough petals for multiple images.

How to Grow: Zinnias grow easily from seed, sown directly in the garden after the threat of frost has passed. (Seedlings started indoors are difficult to transplant into the garden, so it's best to sow the seed outdoors.) Zinnias grow best in full sun, in fertile, well-drained soil that's been amended with organic matter. The plants are subject to rot and fungus, so be sure to allow for good air circulation when planting. Water and fertilize the plants frequently and thoroughly during the growing season. Zinnias are considered hardy and easy to grow and will reward you with blooms over a long period.

How to Hammer: Single blossoms, such as those from *Z. haageana,* can be hammered as a whole. Clip the blossom off the stem and place face down on fabric that is on paper towels. Carefully place another paper towel over the blossom, poking the paper through the hard, green center part. Starting on the outside edges, carefully hammer the petals first, then hammer the center part gently. Often, as you hammer the petals, the center part will release its pigment.

Double or semi-double flowers (*Z. elegans*) must be taken apart and hammered one petal at a time. Place a paper towel underneath your fabric, then tape down each petal to keep it securely in place. Put plastic wrap or another paper towel on top of the petals and hammer.

Quick Reference Chart

Part of the fun (and frustration) of pounding flowers is that some plants produce a perfect image and others won't work at all—some work on one type of fabric or paper, while others work better on a different material. Here is a handy reference chart to let you know, at a glance, the plants that worked best for me. Use this guide as a jumping off point for your own experiments. *Note:* When you hammer images onto silk, always use extra paper towels under the fabric and on top of the plant material unless the plant material is dry.

PLANT	LINEN	WOOL	COTTON	SILK	WATERCOLOR PAPER
ASPARAGUS FERN*	● not as sharp as on cotton	● deep tones but flowed together more than on other fabrics	● sharp edges	●	●
ASTER	● nice, clear purple color	● deep tones; turned a bit pink	● turned a bit muddy	● nice tones	●
BALLOON FLOWER	● nice, crisp transfer; colors are slightly rosy purple	● deep tones, more gray	● best fabric for transfers; veins show up well	● nice tones for silk	● not solid colors but enough vein coloration to make an airy impression

* An asterisk indicates that I used leaves, not flowers, for my tests.

Quick Reference Chart

PLANT	LINEN	WOOL	COTTON	SILK	WATERCOLOR PAPER
BEE BALM	●	● rich, deep red	●	●	● colors not as vivid and bracts seem to "squirt" pigments
BEGONIA, WAX	● very pale transfer	● pink blossom turned purple	● stayed pink	●	●
BLACKBERRY LILY	● best fabric for transfer; dark red dots show up well; crisp edges to petals; good color	● color turned out a bit pinkish; dots don't show up	● good transfer; dots show up well, though colors a little faded	●	●
BUTTER DAISY	● pale yellow blossoms	● best fabric for transfer; dark yellow tones; will fade	● deeper tones than on linen	●	● yellow turns a little muddy, but holds color
CARROT TOPS*	● images are a bit washed out	● excellent, dark, deep tones	●	● very nice transfer; deepest pigment tones are on leaf edges	● deepest tones on leaf edges; practice first to see if you like the effect
CALADIUM*	● nice clear tones	● tones are deepest on this fabric	● good transfer	● good transfer	● gives a vague impression, not a complete transfer, but still appealing
CHRYSANTHEMUM	● very nice transfer with the truest color of all fabrics	● nice deep tones; turned darker than actual flower color	● color turned a bit muddy	● purple petals turned light pink	●
CLEOME	● petals are light	● best fabric for transfer; petals show up well	● pink petals turned a bit muddy, but showed up well	● petals too faint to be useful, though stamen transferred well	● for stamen only
COLEUS*	● good crisp edges; nice color transfer	● darker tones, more pronounced veins	●	● light colors but distinct enough for veins to show	●

	● good transfer	● okay transfer	● poor transfer

Quick Reference Chart

PLANT	LINEN	WOOL	COTTON	SILK	WATERCOLOR PAPER
COREOPSIS	● bright color; butternut tones	● deep yellow	● a bit muddy, not as clear as on other fabrics	● very good color	● turns dark butternut yellow with lots of brown, but a pleasant color
COSMOS	● purplish-pink transfer; good crisp lines; veins in petals show	● brings out deepest tones, almost purple-black for darker petals; practice on scraps to get the shade you want	● good, clear transfer; more detail than on linen, though colors aren't quite as clear and bright	● one of the best flowers to transfer on silk; colors are bright and lines are crisp and even, though images fade faster than on other fabrics	●
DAHLIA (PINK PETALS)	● edges a little fuzzy	● dark purple-pink tones, nice details	● slightly gray, good details	● nice, clear pink tone	● pink turns purple
DIANTHUS	● not my favorite; petals faded a bit at the tips	● good color	● magenta petals transferred perfectly; deep purple	● one of the best flowers to transfer on silk; notched edges showed up beautifully with good color	● color turned out purplish and a bit muddy, but nice, deep tone
DILL*	● not as bright or "solid" looking as on other fabric	● very nice transfer, though turns brown with age	● nicer tones and longer-lasting image than on wool	● a little light, but still attractive for many designs	● negative image (plant is outlined in pigment, with no pigment inside the image)
DOGWOOD, PINK	● nice clear pink	● rich, deep pink	● turns a bit muddy	● faint, but crisp transfer	●
FERNS*	● good transfer but not the most "solid" looking	● excellent transfer; green color lasts longer than on other fabrics	●	●	● nice transfer, but turns brown almost immediately
GERBER DAISY	●	● red turned dark; petals turned dark brown on untreated wool	● red turned a bit muddy brown	● one of the best winter flowers for transferring; red turned pinkish	●

Quick Reference Chart

PLANT	LINEN	WOOL	COTTON	SILK	WATERCOLOR PAPER
GRAPE, MUSCADINE*	●	●	●	●	●
HOLLYHOCK, MINI	● colors were a little pale	● good transfer with rich, deep colors	● crisp lines and good colors	● pale impression	●
IMPATIENS (SALMON COLORED)	● muddy pink color	● deep transfer, closest to original color; good leaf transfer	● colors were a bit muddy, but not as much as on linen; good leaf transfer	● beautiful transfer, more pink than orange; leaf "squirted" a bit	●
IRIS, DUTCH	● nice clear transfer	● deep colors	● colors not as clear as on linen, nor as deep as on wool	● very light colors and fuzzy edges	●
IRONWEED	● light lavender–pink transfer, fades toward center	● excellent transfer; leaf darkens and flowers are intense pink	● flowers are pink on edges, fading toward center; leaf transfers well, with clear veins	● very nice transfer; most intense flower color toward edges; leaf transfers well	● very nice transfer; color more true to purple than on fabric; good color into the center; did not fade as with fabrics
IVY, ENGLISH*	● transfer looks a bit faded	● green takes on a brownish tint	● good, crisp lines	● one of the better greens to use on silk	●
KUDZU	● tones are a bit light and fabric threads aren't thoroughly covered	● deep tones; nice venation	● not a thorough saturation of color, but better than on linen	● very nice transfer; crisp edges and good venation	● use thin layer of cotton cloth on top instead of paper towel
LARKSPUR	●	● deepest tones and most distinct green color	●	● good impression, though much lighter than on other fabrics	● excellent dark blue color

● good transfer	● okay transfer	● poor transfer

Quick Reference Chart

PLANT	LINEN	WOOL	COTTON	SILK	WATERCOLOR PAPER
LOBELIA	● excellent transfer; saturates all threads	● excellent transfer; color turns a bit purple but good, deep tones	● excellent transfer; clear blue color	● not quite as crisp as with other fabrics, but intense color for silk	● very nice blue
LOROPETALUM* (MAROON LEAF)	● deep pink transfer	● deep maroon transfer	● medium maroon transfer, with shades of green throughout	● light transfer with good, clean edges; nice blends of pink and green	● bluish-purple transfer, not nearly as red as on fabrics
MAPLE, JAPANESE*	● bright red leaf turned pink-maroon; green parts looked a bit brown	● very good, crisp transfer; nice colors, deeper tones	● similar to linen transfer; more difficult to get pigments to transfer thoroughly	● lines less crisp, but nice transfer; colors not as bright as on other fabrics	●
MARIGOLD	● almost too light; nice colors but looks faded	● bright yellow tones	● a little pale	● leaf transfers better than flower, which is quite pale	● excellent transfer; great for paper projects
MOSS PINK	● crisp, with good, deep colors; holds pink color better than on other fabrics, but still quite purple	● not as deep as with other blossoms on wool, but good, crisp lines	● color has more gray tones than on wool or linen	● takes on a lavender color, but a good transfer	● good color and crisp edges
NANDINA*	● green leaves transfer well; crimson leaves transfer unevenly	● green leaves transfer well; crimson leaves turn maroon	● green leaves transfer well; crimson leaves not satisfactory	●	● green leaves transfer very well; crimson leaves not satisfactory
NIGELLA	● beautiful impression; blue blossoms have a purple tint	● deep, rich tones; blue blossoms have a green tint	● good color from both petals and leaves	● nice impression, though blue petals are pale and indistinct; leaves transfer well	●
OXALIS, PINK	●	● good, deep tone for leaf	● nice pink color; holds pigments well	●	● pink turns lavender to gray, but edges are crisp

Quick Reference Chart

PLANT	LINEN	WOOL	COTTON	SILK	WATERCOLOR PAPER
PANSY (PINK-PURPLE FLOWERS)	● nice vein details; good color	● rich colors, but not as detailed as on linen	● nice detail, but colors not as deep or as true as on linen	● turns purple; not much detail, but sharp edges	● colors a bit muddy; edges aren't even
PERIWINKLE, ROSE	● turned a fairly deep purple-pink	● turned a bit purple, but not as much as on linen	● kept the pink color best, though transfer not as vivid as original flower	● good transfer; nice purple-pink, though light	● turned dark blue-purple
PETUNIA	● colors a little pale; lines not distinct	● good, rich tones	● best fabric for transfer; nice colors; veins distinct in petals	● very pale	● wonderful transfer; good color tones, nice edges
PHLOX	● young flower hammers more true to color; older flower is distinct lavender color	● rich tones; older blossom is purple, young blossom is blue	● blossom is gray; looks slightly muddy	●	● good image, though pink blossoms are slightly muddy purple
PHLOX, BLUE	● good transfer; clear, blue color	● deeper tones; color a bit purple	● good transfer; color is lighter with gray in it	● clear blue color; crisp outer lines	●
PINCUSHION FLOWER (BLUE)	● good transfer; nice rosy-purple color	● much pinker than actual flower	● blue-gray color	● soft, slightly blurry transfer; pale color	●
PLUMBAGO	● light purplish-blue	● best fabric for transfer; center veins of petals show up; color is purple-gray	● very gray tones	●	●
PRIMROSE (PINK)	● good, clear color; nice, crisp lines	● deep pink tones; nice lines; long-lasting	● turns a muddy color that worsens with age	●	●

● good transfer   ● okay transfer   ● poor transfer

180 ❀ THE ART AND CRAFT OF POUNDING FLOWERS

Quick Reference Chart

PLANT	LINEN	WOOL	COTTON	SILK	WATERCOLOR PAPER
PRIMROSE (RED)	● very nice transfer with good color	● rich, deep tones	● a bit brown but still attractive	● fades, leaving edge of dark brown-red	●
QUEEN ANNE'S LACE	● good, clear, long-lasting impression	● very dark, intense green; great detail (leave enough spaces to see individual stems so it doesn't transfer as a green blob)	● best fabric for transfer; great depth to impression; flowering stems seem to sit on top of the leaves	● slightly fuzzy impression	●
REDBUD*	●	● nice deep tones with distinctive veins that look white against dark green leaf	● most distinctive veining; but hard to get an even transfer	● beautiful color	●
ROSE, MINI (PINK)	● clear color and crisp edges	● not as crisp as on linen or cotton, but color is deeper	● slightly muddy color	● very light but nice pastel color	●
ROSE OF SHARON (PINK)	● beautiful clear, lilac color	● deeper tones, more pinkish than on linen	● more gray tones in petal; attractive shade but not true to plant color	● faint transfer, but nice color	● color not great; transfer not crisp
SASSAFRAS*	● not as "solid" looking as on other fabrics	● best fabric for transfer; nice, deep tones; good venation	● great transfer with distinct veins	● beautiful colors; nice, crisp edges	● a very faint transfer, but nice
SOURWOOD*	● gorgeous transfer; lime green and deep red with white venation; definite pinkish tones	● deep rich tones; colors darker than on linen; images are stiff, making this a bit difficult to use to decorate clothing	● red turns a bit pink-purple; not as nice a transfer as on other fabrics	● wonderful transfer; good blend and contrast of colors; better than on wool because fabric stays supple	● muddy red with few details; hammers best if leaf is taped down

QUICK REFERENCE CHART ❀ 181

Quick Reference Chart

PLANT	LINEN	WOOL	COTTON	SILK	WATERCOLOR PAPER
STOKES ASTER	● definite pinkish tones	● beautiful, deep salmon-pink	● orange-pink transfer	●	●
SUMAC, STAGHORN*	● dark red transfer; color somewhat uneven	● good, crisp transfer; color turns a bit orange	● colors are a bit purplish; good vein detail	● pinkish tones	● bright red leaf transferred dull purple
SWEET GUM*	● very nice image; crisp edges; good venation	● purple color appeared redder than on linen	● purple turned muddy	● nice clear colors; good display of veins	●
SWITCH GRASS*	●	● deep tones	●	● faint, but usable	●
VERBENA (BRIGHT PINK)	● best fabric for transfer; intense colors	● slightly orange tones	● a bit gray in the center	● great transfer; very intense colors for silk	● colors slightly purple-gray
VINCA	● great dark blue transfer; crisp edges	● good dark tone; a bit lighter than on linen	● blue takes on a gray tone	● blue takes on a green tint	● colors aren't always good
VIOLA	●	● purplish tones look a bit rosy pink; veins in petals are very good	● purple stays true; image stays bright if protected from sunlight	● fainter transfer than on other fabrics	● best if green parts are removed before hammering
VIRGINIA CREEPER*	● very nice, good rich colors	● faded and a bit muddy	● colors a bit pink-brown	●	●
WISTERIA	● a bit purplish	● good, deep tones that don't fade as quickly as on other fabrics	● blue turns a bit muddy with age	● clear blue-purple	●
ZINNIA (SALMON-COLORED Z. ELEGANS)	● turns a bit brown with age	● great transfer; rich tones	● very nice transfer; soft bright colors	● pale but good for silk	●
ZINNIA (ORANGE Z. LINEARIS)	● good yellow-orange color	● nice, rich deep orange tones	● orange turned a bit brown toward center	● colors not as intense as on other fabrics	

● good transfer	● okay transfer	● poor transfer